TAKING CHARGE
IN TODAY'S ECONOMY
Secrets of Credit Card Processing Revealed

By Mariusz Kapturski

Copyright © 2009
by Mariusz Kapturski
edited by Terry Golway, Jette England and Dr. Donna Koch

All rights reserved.
No part of this book may be reproduced in any form.

Published by Kean University Press
Kean University, 1000 Morris Avenue, Union, New Jersey 07083
www.kean.edu

Printed in the United States of America

ISBN 978-1-61623-366-2

FORWORD

There are many books about sales, but not one about credit card processing, which is one of the most important industries in today's high-tech, knowledge-based economy. We're all affected in one way or another by this intensely competitive field, yet it has surprisingly inspired very little research. This book will likely change that. For the first time merchants, banks, and consumers will have a reference guide to the world of electronic payments.

My years in the business have convinced me that this field also offers great opportunities to motivated, hard-working people who are ready to grasp the chance at success. If you're looking to start a new career, or if you've fallen victim to today's hard economic times, this book may help you reboot your career and your life. If you are a merchant, this book will help you understand the complexities of an industry that affects millions of businesses, like yours everyday. As a sales person, you will be detailed on key issues that will ultimately affect your performance.

If you decide to buy this book, you will explore the value of merchant banking, recent governmental regulations and its impact on merchants and consumers alike. In addition, you will be exposed to a great deal of interesting and up to date information about the electronic payment industry. I will also share with you my own experiences, sales techniques and strategies which I have used in the field and the secrets of getting the best possible deals for your potential clients and business owners.

Most processors will not like me freely sharing this information with the public. However, I would like that every merchant be treated fairly and for them to understand what they are actually paying for, so that they can make a well-informed decision about choosing their credit card processor. Salespeople will also gain a new perspective on how to choose their ISO, or employer in order to maximize their profit earnings. This book will teach you the tricks to reading between the lines even in the likelihood that those lines may sometimes intentionally be deleted.

*To my parents: Wieslaw and Danuta Kapturskich
and to my wife Donna.*

CONTENTS

Introduction 2
Global Challenges
   Merchant banking as part of the free market
   Brief overview

CHAPTER ONE 7
   Breaking Into Sales
   Introduction to merchant banking
   Coming back hard
   Selling on my own

CHAPTER TWO 17
   Understanding the Interchange Fees and More
   How the transaction is authorized
   Pricing plans

CHAPTER THREE 33
   Reading the Statements
   Field training
   Sales calls

CHAPTER FOUR 61
   Signing Up a Bank
   Networking in the community
   Agent-ISO agreement

CHAPTER FIVE 71
   You are the Boss, Becoming an ISO
   And now some numbers
   My plan to change merchant banking
   Seize the opportunity

CHAPTER SIX 89
   The Australian Reform of Credit Card Payments
   The future of merchant banking
   Let's analyze the arguments
   After word

Introduction

Merchant banking is one of the most fascinating pieces of our economy. The electronic payment industry is only about 25 years old and in that short period of time, it has transformed the global economy. Though we take it for granted, it is hard for us to imagine not being able to use a credit card for purchases, especially when we are low on cash. Not only have consumers become dependent on this system of payment, but banks generate extra revenue from interchange fees, and merchants make billions of dollars because their customers rely extensively on electronic purchases.

In the past, credit card transactions were processed using paper tickets and voice authorizations. Merchants then lined up with those tickets at the bank to deposit their credit card sales. Of course, today technology for the most part has eliminated manual processing. Nowadays technology is constantly changing and implementing new innovative electronic systems and securities. There are different software and point of sale terminals that are widely available to the merchants. Merchants can use standard phone lines, wireless communication, cash registers with attached card readers and software with Internet connections.

Credit and debit cards make our lives so much easier because of their convenience. But most people have no idea how the system works, or how complex this seemingly simple process truly is. Nor have we thought about who actually processes these transactions for us. There are a lot of things associated with it. We will be addressing these issues in the following chapters.

Global challenges

With the economic challenges of our times and many people losing their jobs every day, the problems that we face are overwhelming. If we can act together, we are more likely to find the way to resolve our global economic problems through cooperation. The question is: Will it be possible for big financial institutions to work together, create an alternative for government spending and control, redirect some of the profit they generate into the private sector and use it for new job creation and repair this broken and corrupt financial system before it completely collapses? Will the governments cooperate with the private sector to solve our global challenges or will they try to gain complete control and dictate the economy?

Ghulam Umar, a political analyst from Pakistan wrote: *"The growing interdependence of the world has given rise to a series of global problems that individual states can no longer resolve by themselves. Only through worldwide cooperation can we cope with the growing dangers and challenges that mankind faces"*. Today's weak global economy is one of those challenges that need to be addressed. It may be resolved by individual nations cooperating with their financial institutions that have the resources and finances to deal with poverty. Wealth is created not through confiscation of power and irresponsibly spent by bureaucrats. If we want to strengthen our economy we need to avoid special interests groups and government intervention. We can do that by directly injecting finances into our private sector and oppose the government expansion, which for the most parts only confiscates what we produce. Cooperation between government and financial institutions might be the best option.

Merchant banking as part of the free market

> *"The free market is a market governed by the laws of supply and demand, free of government intervention and regulation except for instances in which government is maintaining the legal system and protecting private property rights. The free market is also free of private force and fraud where property rights are voluntarily exchanged at the price arranged solely by the mutual consent of sellers and buyers"* – Free Encyclopedia.

The merchant banking industry is still one of a very few markets where many individual businesses can thrive on their own without government intervention. The simple act of owning a credit card allows consumers to participate in this free market, where millions of merchants and cardholders across the globe are engaged in the exchange of goods and services for credit.

The free market gives us opportunities. Opportunity creates competition, competition leads to creativity, creativity leads to invention, invention leads to new job creation, new job creation leads to productivity. You get the idea. This perpetual system keeps our free markets from falling into stagnation rendering opportunities for people like you and I to succeed as business entrepreneurs.

> *"The most important single central fact about a free market is that no exchange takes place unless both parties benefit."* – Milton Friedman

Let me tell you who benefits from the electronic payments. Here is the list:
1. The card issuers,
2. Banks and credit unions,
3. Merchants whose revenue increases by accepting this payment method,
4. Cardholders who can afford goods and services by borrowing money through credit cards,
5. Acquirers and processors,
6. Everybody who works in this industry from the customer service to sales,
7. Finally - the government who collect taxes on all the transactions that take place on the free market – through sales tax or income tax.

As you can see, this industry is a huge contributor to our society.

Are you now ready to learn about the payment industry? Are you ready to absorb the information?

Ok, lets get started.

Brief overview

Around seven years ago I was unfamiliar with merchant services and did not even know what the credit card terminal was. Like most consumers, I thought that the bank takes care of the entire process once the credit card has been swiped. Nothing can be further from the truth. The bank has very little if anything to do with the processing part. In most cases, the bank has an established relationship with an Independent Sales Organization or an acquirer and sends them only a referral. The ISO takes it from there: the application, the programming of the terminal and the customer service. The only thing that the bank does is make money on the referral. How? The bank gets to keep a percentage of the profit that the ISO generates from the account on a monthly basis. Usually it affects the price. You as a merchant have to pay a higher price using your local bank as a "processor".

What is an ISO? I will explain that later, and I will tell you how to become an ISO and what needs to be done to be a successful ISO. I will also share with you all the secrets associated with the credit card processing industry. There are many wise men out there who have been working in electronic payments for a very long time and who know more than I do. I have been exploring this industry only for a little more than three years, but I will share with you all of my experiences and the things that I learned about electronic payments along the way.

In the following chapters you will find: sales tips and techniques, industry jargon and definitions, a lot of mathematical graphs and charts, merchants' and issuers' views on potential industry regulations and something extra special that I want to share with you. That is the Bible, my "moral compass" which you can use at liberty if you choose to help you succeed in this business as well. Why the Bible's advice?

> "All Scripture is inspired of God and beneficial for teaching, for setting things straight, for disciplining in righteousness, that the man of god may be fully competent, completely equipped for every good work" (2 Timothy 3:16,17).

In today's world, which seems to have lost its moral bearings and is often driven by greed and corruption, the Bible contains wisdom and knowledge on how to deal with those things and be successful.

Greed, selfishness, corruption, jealousy, abuse of power - this is what drives our world today, *"But know this, that in the last days critical times hard to deal with will be here. For men will be lovers of themselves, lovers of money, self-assuming, haughty, blasphemers, disobedient to parents, unthankful, disloyal, having no natural affection, not open to any agreement, slanderers, without self-control, fierce, without love of goodness, betrayers, headstrong, puffed up with pride, lovers of pleasures rather than lovers of God, having a form of godly devotion but proving false to its powers, and from this turn away"* (2 Timothy 3:1-5).

CHAPTER ONE

BREAKING INTO SALES

Many of you probably have read several books about sales. But I think it is always good to learn a new perspective. Sales requires special skills, but if you do not have them, don't worry - they can be learned and developed through practice, like a good golf swing. Training is crucial. You need to be patient when many merchants tell you no. To fully understand the power of your sales skills, first you will need to overcome your fears. What fears? You'll learn quickly enough. You'll know what it's like to skip a merchant's door because you fear rejection. It's a common feeling, but you have to overcome it. Never skip any door. Visit every merchant location on your path. The best practice is actually going out and trying to make the sale.

You could say that I've been around a salesman all my life as my father was a salesman. He started selling groceries in Poland, in my native town Radom, around 15 years ago. He was an unforgettable sight as he cycled from store to store with his bread, pizza pies and donuts. He was a natural salesman. He could talk anybody in to buying anything from him - even if they didn't need what he was selling. Now that's the mark of a genius! On some days, he sold 200 loaves of bread, 200 pizza pies and more than 300 donuts. I was the eldest sibling in my family, so he often took me to help him. He needed help. We didn't have a car, and, to tell you the truth, I was very embarrassed riding on a bike with a big heavy trunk at the back, with three or four boxes full of bread, rolls and donuts.

First lesson. *Learn to be confident and like what you do.*

My father was a character. He always talked to everybody on the street, which did not make it any easier for me to ride with him. Just imagine that. Me, at the age of 15, on the bike after school, with all the boxes at the back driving on the street trying to sell bread and donuts, being seen by all of my friends who later made fun of me. Strangers began to recognize me as I made my rounds with my father. I'd wake up at four in the morning, go to the bakery, pick up the donuts, sell them at the factory gates - all before I went to school. And people loved it! In the old good days I could sell about 200 donuts in an hour!

I did very well, but then the business became more competitive as the other people opened up their own bread routes. Many more people started to do the same thing. But it always came down to who was there first - who was willing to work the hardest, who was willing to make the sacrifices necessary to succeed in a competitive market.

My father was a very innovative man. He was always coming up with new kinds of donuts that somehow drove the customers to us. And he always somehow talked the bakery into making a new style donut for him. This was one of the most important lessons for me. *Be innovative.* If you want to succeed, do something different. Make your own brand! It worked for some time. What, you might ask, does any of this have to do with merchant banking? Well, it's really all about sales, and about learning a sales philosophy before actually dealing with the complexities of the industry. Even if you already are in sales, you can learn from my perspective, just as I can learn from yours. I learn new things every day from the people around me.

Here is another lesson: *Be open for new knowledge, never think that you know everything.* Back to my days as a donut salesman: at one point, the other bakeries started making better donuts than the one my father sold. Believe me, I know - I tried them. My father had to come up with something new. And he did. He started to make a donuts with new kind of filling. And they sold very well. Besides that, he talked a lot about his donuts. Nothing sells a product better than talking to your customers. Just imagine talking to your customers and making jokes about your product all the time. Actually, my father didn't simply talk - he shouted. He talked at the top of his lungs, to anybody who would listen (and even some who didn't). I was with him at parking lots and bus stations, and when I heard him give his pitch, I wanted to hide under a rock. I was embarrassed, but now I realize that those people - those potential customers - actually listened to my father. And he made the sale.

If you are a good talker, boy, you can sell! That leads to another important lesson - *Talking to your customer*. And not only that. You have to listen, too. Especially when your customers have a complaint. You can't shrug it off - you have to act. Give them a discount. That almost always works!

This was my introduction to the sales. I became a very confident donut seller! As times continued to change and competition became tougher, I had to adapt. I found myself visiting factories every morning to sell the same number of donuts I sold outside one. First, I visited the factory which opened the earliest. I had to manage my time there - sometimes I had to leave a little early even though I lost a few customers that way. I knew that in the other location I could easily make up for the difference and sell an extra fifty donuts or more. Another lesson. *Learn to manage your options and time!* The sooner you master that skill, the better off you will be in the future. We often have to make difficult choices.

Some of the customers from the first location learned to come earlier to buy donuts from me. When I had to leave early, I was honest with them. I explained that I had to hustle to beat my competition. They understood. Some of them patronized my competitors, who came after I left, but they always came back to me

When I was 18, I started to sell strawberries in the summer time during the school break. I had a car, and drove 50 miles to buy strawberries directly from the field. Eventually I bought many small baskets that they could not fit in my car anymore. I drove back to my home town and sold them in front of the supermarkets. I was making good money by selling about 250 baskets a day. But I soon realized that I might make more money by just transporting those strawberries and letting somebody else sell them at different locations. I found two people who bought 200 baskets from me every day, and I made a second trip to buy 150 for myself. Volume! This is another secret of being successful in sales. When it comes to the merchant banking it is no different. *You make money on volume*. The more money you process, the more you make.

I was selling my own strawberries in different locations, so I was not competing with those who bought my strawberries wholesale. It was easy. I spoke to the owner of the field a day before to make an arrangement to pick up 400 boxes in the morning and then another 200 at noon. Of course I was always negotiating the price because I was buying a lot. If I did not get a good price, I went somewhere else where I got a discount. That was another lesson. *Learn to negotiate*. Don't be afraid to take the risk. If you can't buy it cheaper somewhere else, pay the same price. But the next time when you come back to the original place you will get a discount for sure. Why? Because the guy will think that you can get a better price somewhere else and he will not want to lose a customer. I learned that you make money on volume, not on a single item. Sell quickly and sell a lot. That's my philosophy. This is how most of the big companies work in today's market. *Volume.*

So what are the keys to a successful sales career? B*e innovative, be confident, negotiate, overcome and adapt to the new situation.* And don't forget about discipline. Discipline is a very important factor on the way to the success. If you can learn and apply all above, selling merchant banking will be so much easier.

And now, finally we will enter the world of electronic payments. While I'll keep focus on merchant banking, I can't forget my roots as kid who sold donuts and strawberries. The lessons of my past have helped me sell merchant banking products. People say we should learn from our own mistakes. It's true, but why shouldn't we also learn from the experience - and mistakes - of other people? Well, I've just shared some of mine insights with you. If you will follow my advice it will help you to get where you want to be much faster.

Introduction to merchant banking

After I graduated college in Poland I had an opportunity to come to United States, and I did in March of 2001. That is where my first encounter with the merchant banking took place. It was about seven years ago in New Jersey. I was a college student trying to make some money on the weekends working construction with my friends. One day I got a phone call from a broker I knew. He said that one of his friends, who was the CEO and founder of a merchant service company needed some guys who could do some work on his house.

We met him on the weekend and he asked us if we could start immediately. We did, and after a long weekend he decided to hire only me.

I asked him why, and he told me that I had a work ethic and commitment that he rarely seen before. That's how I began a very important friendship and business relationship, one which unknowingly at that time helped launch my current career.

Over the next couple of days we started talking about his business - merchant banking. I always liked the idea of sales and numbers, so immediately I was very interested in it. During the next three months I got to know his family and occasionally at the dinner table we began engaging in conversations about the industry. He taught me the basics, which initially was somewhat hard to understand.

Not only was I trying to learn English, but I was also exposed to a new set of vocabulary that was very foreign to me.

Finally, I decided to try merchant banking for myself. I persuaded my friend to come with me as I tried to sign up my very first account. It was a dentist's office where I was a patient. We arranged an appointment with the dentist who I approached with the idea during one of my visits. We showed up and signed a deal in 10 minutes. This is not a typical encounter, let me assure you. It just so happened that my first client was unhappy with his current processor and I was at the right place at the right time. Hopefully you will have a similar experience at some point, but do not count on it to be with your first sales attempt. Later we sent somebody there to reprogram the credit card terminal and I had my very first account, which I processed for till this very day.

Two weeks later, with some newly acquired theoretical knowledge I decided to try my luck again. I packed the basics needed in this industry: a briefcase with applications, Schedule A's - pricing lists, notebook, three pens and the most important piece - a calculator. And I was ready to go. The first territory I hit was a Polish section in Brooklyn, N.Y. I figured that if I had yet to master the industry I would at least have a very receptive audience as my potential clients spoke Polish, which is my native language. When I approached my first potential customer I looked at the credit card terminal, asked for the owner and than said to him: "Do you see this machine? That is what I am doing! I can get you a much better deal. Just sign the paper here and I will come back to fix your terminal".

Looking back at my first sales presentation when I was barely able to distinguish the difference between two credit card terminals and haven't even realized that there were over 20 different types of them I was astonished that I even left my house, never mind trying to sell my product. Needles to say, I was not as well-received as I hoped I would be. After I visited about 10 locations using the same approach, I realized that I needed a lot more than just my enthusiasm and basic knowledge. I couldn't jump over certain hurdles without mastering the basics. But I refused to give up. I spent two more days visiting about 50 locations trying to close at least one account. It did not work. So back to the drowning board it was.

I know one thing. If you don't quit after the early embarrassments, you may succeed in sales. Most newcomers quit after an early disaster or embarrassment. They simply can't overcome their fears and can't close a deal. You just have to keep moving forward and finally you'll gain your confidence and experience and sign your first merchant account. Learn, overcome and adapt. If you cannot do it, you will not survive it this industry.

About three months later my credit card mentor decided to move out of New Jersey and my short adventure with merchant banking sales seemed as though it was coming to an end. At least for a short while. Not that I wanted it to end. In fact, I tried to find training seminars, books - anything that might help me pursue this new career. But I found nothing. I was unable to make another sale without additional training. That's when I realized how important field training is. I'll expand on that later.

Coming back hard!

After a long break from sales I decided that I not only missed the business but I also longed to see my friend and mentor. It just so happened that three years later, while I was talking to my barber, he was complaining about the excessive fees the he had to pay to his credit card processor. I realized that I could help him, so I reached out to my old friend in Idaho. I decided that my trip out to Idaho would be for both, pleasure and business. This time I was more ready than ever to tackle the industry once again from a fresh perspective.

My friend's office had changed quite a bit since I visited it three years earlier. I was pleased to see that his business expanded and he had eight employees who worked at the office in addition to his growing sales force. I got to work right away. I spent two eight hour days with his office manager, who taught me all the details of pricing, applications, interchange fees and other things about merchant banking that I needed to know before I began selling again. I had to digest a lot of information in a short period of time. After I learned the pricing plans that were available, I decided that my signature pricing plan would be something called interchange pass through pricing. This plan was easy to understand and very fair for the merchant. I will explain this plan later.

I was studying really hard but I realized one more thing from my past experience. I needed somebody who could show me a practical part of selling the merchant banking. Somebody who could drive with me on a field to show me how to actually close a deal. Without that, all my sales experience would not work and the long hours spent with office manager would be just a waste of time. I knew the product, I knew the price and pricing plans. But I did not know how to successfully sign a deal. My friend promised, that his National Sales Manager would come to New Jersey three weeks after I returned from Idaho, to give me some guidance in the field. After I found out about the opportunities that lay ahead of me in this industry I could not wait to start selling again.

On my flight back home my friend gave me the materials that I needed to better understand and recap what I learned over the past week. I was reading a publication called The Green Sheet, which I got from him, and the sales book to improve my sales skills. The Green Sheet is a free publication with information about the electronic payments. It is accessible and freely available to everyone who signs up via internet or mailing to receive it. This magazine contains up to date information on current changes in the industry as well as employment opportunities.

Three weeks later as promised, my friend's national sales manger arrived in New Jersey from Idaho. He was a sharp young fellow in his early 30s, and he was supremely confident about his sales skills. I drove him to a hotel near my house, and within minutes, he was making a sale - to the hotel managers. He introduced himself to the staff, asked for the manager and when the manger showed up, he started the sale. That's how it is done - he sad. Easy. Just be confident and know what you are talking about. For the next ten days we visited about 200 different locations and closed 3 deals. It was very hard work. We were leaving my house at 7:30 a.m. and returning at 7 p.m. It was a lot of driving and going back to the same places many times. During this time I had learned how to read the statements and how to make a spreadsheet to compare the discount rates. I watched my field trainer and learned. Observation is a crucial component of learning. Watch, listen, learn and apply! After three days of driving with the National Sales Manager, I asked him if I could try to make a sale. He agreed. I simply tried to mimic his approach with the client and used the same dialog with the same confidence that he had. I must admit, that I had not expected that selling merchant banking might be so hard. It seemed much easier than it was. So, I had my first ten days of training. It wasn't much, but it was enough for me to acquaint myself with the hands on part pf selling. I got the field training that I lacked in the past and my confidence back, and this was what I needed. The National Sales Manager went back to Idaho and I started a new chapter in my career, selling on my own.

Selling on my own

It was January. Cold outside. But I was working hard. My first month was very impressive. I managed my time well, kept good notes and was able to open eight merchant accounts! I didn't really know how well I was doing because I had no comparison. I found out later from the regional sales director from First Data that for most sales people it is difficult to close more than two deals in the first month. At this point I knew that I was on the right track.

The next month was even better. I brought to my ISO eleven new merchant accounts! And I did not stop there. In the full year, working just part time I managed to close 72 accounts in the metropolitan area, totaling around 25,000 transactions a month and monthly processing volume of around $1,2 million.

My residuals started to grow slowly, and at the end of the year I was ready to explore this industry full time. Here is an example how much you can make in your first couple of months in this industry if you perform. It is simple mathematics. If you open 20 accounts in first three months with monthly volume of 300,000 you make about $450 a month in the third month if you collect just straight residuals. If you decide to give up some of your residuals for upfront bonuses you may make more money in the first months but it is not a good deal for you in a long run.

You get paid monthly, not weekly and the checks for January come in March. If you can sell some equipment in a meantime, your check might be bigger. This is how it works in this industry. Your income keeps growing parallel with your portfolio. But it is important to remember that the first months can be difficult, if you do not have upfront bonuses. It is simply not enough to pay the bills. Plus you get no reimbursement. You are on your own. You make a sale, you make a buck; you do not, you starve. That is why most of the sales people in this industry quit after the first year. Not only do they struggle to make a sale, but there is not enough income to cover their expenses. And you have to pay for gas and the phone bill. Yes, that is right! - your ISO does not cover your travel costs and business expenses.

You need to understand that you build your portfolio slowly, year by year, and if you are patient and dedicated to your profession, and you consistently bring four to five accounts a month, you will succeed. After three years of hard work you might have around 200 accounts open, and your portfolio might bring you a good income. Very good income. All you will need to do then is to manage it and occasionally open two or three accounts a month to keep it growing. But if you are like me, you are not satisfied with that. You will keep working and keep bringing those five accounts a month or more, and your portfolio after six years of hard work might have at least 300 accounts or more. Then your monthly income would be about +/- $10,000 a month, depending on how you price your merchant accounts. It all depends on how hard you are willing to work to get there. I know people who got to that point in three years. Those who think that they can make millions over night will be disappointed. In my first year I was still trying to understand and to learn this unbelievably fascinating industry, and my income was not too impressive.

I was looking for more clues to understand the credit card processing and the pricing structure. My ISO was not too helpful, besides saying that I was doing great. The business requires you to find out information on your own - most people who know this business held onto information and would not share it with me. After many long nights of browsing the Internet and studying the Green Sheet forum, which was the most informative, I learned that there are no books about it, that is why I decided to be the first one to write a book about credit card processing. Every time I found something interesting, I saved it, did more research on it, got the information and send it to my ISO via email to show him that I was learning, and that I cared.

If you want to succeed, you need to know that the money is in sales, not in the office. Even if you have the best office staff, it will not help you to grow your business without good qualified sales people.

My tenacity helped in a different way. After almost a year I finally got access to a website, resource online, that showed me the daily activity of my merchant accounts - the number of transactions processed, the volume of those transactions, and my month to month profit.

The pieces were finally starting to come together.

And now, I am going to walk you through all the darkest secrets of this constantly changing industry. Are you ready for this adventure? Put the seatbelts on. From now on, all you will experience here will be just twists and turns that will keep your adrenaline on a highest level. You will have no choice but only keep reading and ask for more!

CHAPTER TWO

UNDERSTANDING THE INTERCHANGE FEES AND MORE

Interchange. The subject has inspired a good deal of controversy over the few years. What is interchange? In this chapter I will try to answer that question.

Interchange is where everything begins. This is a set of rules that explains the percentage of every dollar that the merchant pays and that the issuing bank gets to keep from every single transaction, and it is **non-negotiable**. Interchange rates vary between 0.7% for some types of cards to almost 3% for the others. It does not say anything about the processors fees, which the merchant has to pay on the top of the interchange rates.

Interchange is a very complicated structure. It includes around 100 different discount rates and transaction fees based on the type of card. It has different rates for: debit cards, rewards cards, credit cards, hand-keyed transactions, transactions over internet, pin based debit transactions, commercial and business cards, corporate cards, card not present transaction, supermarket, small ticket transactions, petroleum and many more.

Lets understand the terms we will be discussing in this chapter.

Issuing bank is the bank that issued the customers credit or debit card.

Processor is the company that handles the processing of credit card transactions for you. The processor has a variety of different service fees, which appear on your monthly statement, and include: statement fees; monthly minimums; annual membership fee; set up account fee; authorization fees or per item rate for every transaction and discount rates, which are higher than interchange. Why so many fees? Simply, because the processor buys those rates from Visa, MasterCard and all debit networks and has to mark it up to make any money. So, for example, monthly statement fee or monthly service fee is usually around $8.00. This fee covers: the service, help desk and statement cost like stamps and envelopes. This fee is in most cases passed to the merchant. ISO pays this fee to the acquirer for every single account open. Depending on the contractual obligations between acquirer and the ISO, this fee might be slightly higher or lower.

Interchange is the largest part of the transaction. Some estimate that the interchange fee is about 80% of every transaction. You probably do not like to pay that much to the bank which simply issued the card. And I agree. Banks are very greedy. Processors are a different story.

They do the job, they process your transactions, they give you a customer service, they protect your business from fraudulent transactions and they make sure that the money gets to your account!

And for all this, the processor takes only about 15% of your fee? Is that fair? Around 5% goes to the acquirer. If this is not enough, every business has to pay different interchange fees.

So if you run a supermarket you pay the lowest fees, if you own a restaurant your fees are higher, if you are in petroleum business you benefit from a special debit rates, if you are in retail your fees are slightly higher and if you are a government you get a discount. Off course different fees reflect different business models, because the risk of fraudulent transactions is higher in one business than in the other. How is that? Well, does your business use a different credit card machine? Or maybe it is a location of your business? How about the clientele? Why doesn't everybody have the same interchange rate?

Ask the card associations. The processor has nothing to do with the interchange. As a matter of fact, the processor has to pay interchange fee to the card associations and mark it up to be able to stay in business.

In my opinion there should be one interchange fee schedule for all the businesses with no exceptions. This would solve many problems that this industry currently is undergoing. The issuing bank charges the merchant for accepting the credit card payments as well as the customer who uses the card. The customer simply borrows the money from that bank to purchase goods from the merchant and pays the percentage fee for that loan. The merchant pays interchange fees. Having a bank is a really good thing — so much income from everywhere! Interchange has been around since the very first card was issued to the cardholder. As The Green Sheet noted on September 8, 2008, "The original intent of interchange was to compensate card issuers for costs and risks associated with extending unsecured credit to cardholders."

But what role does the interchange have now? Don't we have a better security standards and better ways to make sure that customers qualify for credit cards? We do. Why not lower the interchange? Do you know who pays for the rewards that clients get at the end of the year? Merchants. The bank never gives anything for free.

There are around 100 different types of Visa and MasterCard cards on the market and every single one of them has a different price, depending on which bank issued the card and based on the type of card. It is still really hard to understand why every business has to pay different interchange rates. I understand that cards from different issuing banks have a different price. But different interchange rate for different business? Every business should have the same interchange fee schedule.

Here is an example: petroleum debit cost only 0.7%. Retail debit cost is 1.03% for Visa and 1.05% for MasterCard. Big difference. Why can't retail pay the same rate as gas stations for debit, which is 0.7%? Why do only the gas stations can benefit from such a great debit rate?

The same is true of supermarket rates. Those rates are lower than retail rates. Analyze the interchange fees to see the difference. I understand that Internet transactions are more expensive for a simple reason. The card is not present during the transaction and you never know who uses the card. The risk of the fraud is greater. But not to worry. With today's technology, the processor can monitor every transaction in the moment when the card is swiped or even key-entered. The price for those transactions should change soon too. The only risk that we may have then would be a chargeback. It happens quite often when people buy merchandise through the Internet.

Lets get back to interchange.

If you aren't sure about the interchange fee schedule that you got from your ISO, you can find the real interchange rates on the Visa's and MasterCard's websites. Visit Visa.com or MasterCard.com on the Internet and find the word "Merchant" on the top box, then search for interchange rates or fees.

If you are serious about this business, you have to do your homework. Find the interchange rates and learn them, memorize every one of those rates. Why?

1. It will help you to master this business,
2. You will be able to read and understand the monthly merchant statements,
3. You will know the difference between good and bad deal
4. You will know how to price the account

Most of the ISO's never mark up the interchange rates for the sales people who work for them, but some of them have a risk fee that they deduct from your residuals. If your ISO has no liability and the acquirer is responsible for any potential loses, ISO pays an extra 0.0015% or 0.00175% risk fee to the acquirer. Sales people pay the part or full price of the risk fee depending on what their ISO's policy is.

If the ISO takes the risk, there is no risk fees paid to the acquirer, but it is highly possible that the ISO charges salespeople those fees. When this happens, those fees might be higher than the ones paid to the acquirer, for example 0.005%. Everybody is in business to make money.

Why do ISO's or acquirers collect the risk fees? They collect those fees to cover the potential losses in the future if one of the merchants decides to commit the fraud and it is not caught in time.

You have to find a processor who offers you the true interchange rates and also let you know the transaction fee that he pays to the acquirer. This fee is usually around .625 cents and might be slightly higher or lower, depending on the number of transactions that your ISO brings to the acquirer on a monthly basis.

So if you charge 10-cents transaction fee above the interchange, you make around 3 cents on every transaction. Or if your pricing plan is different than cost plus and you charge a 20 cents transaction fee, your profit just from the transaction will also be around 3 cents. It is important to know that. If you have many merchants, and the number of the transactions that you process is about 50,000, you may make nice profit just from transaction fees. You should also have the third-party selling rights on the contract with your processor. I'll explain why later.

Merchants can check the interchange rates too, so they can estimate how much they pay for the service that they are getting from the processor, and decide for themselves if the price they pay for the service they get is worth their hard earned money. It is the price of doing business, but everyone of you, dear merchants should not be paying more than 0.5% for the processing part that you got from your Independent Sales Organization. Usually the bigger the processing volume, the better service price, but this is understandable. You cannot expect that a processor will give the same price to a merchant who is processing $1,000 a month as the one whose monthly processing volume is $200,000.

We will get into the numbers later. But it is important to bear in mind that the processing fees including interchange and service fees that every merchant pays are on average about $2.70 for every $100. Just the service fee is about $0.5. Clearly, the interchange is the largest part of the transaction.

Banks are making billions of dollars per year by collecting the interchange fees from the card associations like Visa and MasterCard. Banks are members of those associations and they dictate the price of interchange. So, don't be angry with your processors. They do not set the rules.

As a merchant, you have to understand that every processor has to register with Visa and MasterCard and pay a fee to be able to use their logos and to get the wholesale pricing. Registration fees are pretty high. It costs about $15,000 a year including the debit networks. ISO's simply resell the product to you with a mark up, so they can cover the registration fees and stay in business. Then, they have to establish a relationship with one of the acquirers like for example First Data or Chase Paymentech, to be able to use their networks for processing the credit card transactions. That is why we have authorization fees or transaction fees. These fees cover the cost of the connection between the credit card terminal, the acquirer and the issuing bank to verify the credit card information and to authorize the transaction.

All of the registration fees are very high, and for most merchants out there it will not be profitable to pay Visa and MasterCard fees just to get the wholesale price, because you would lose a lot of money. And Visa and MasterCard do not sell them directly to the merchant.

It is much better to buy those rates from a processor. The price is slightly higher, but it comes with the service and comfort of having somebody who will always take care of your credit card processing problems if you need help. It saves a lot of headaches.

Accepting the credit cards is a privilege not a right, and not everybody can qualify for it. Usually, merchants with a very low credit score have a difficult time to get approved for it. The privilege of accepting the credit cards usually brings your sales volume up to about 30% or in certain businesses even more than 50%. You pay for the convenience of accepting credit payments and it helps to grow your business.

But isn't the price that you pay for interchange too high? I will try to answer that question in my last two chapters.

Machines often break. It is good to have somebody you can call at any situation to get help when your terminal stops working. If you have a busy location and your terminal stops working you may lose a lot of business before it will be fixed. Service often comes with the price. If you don't know how to read your statement and you need help to understand it - call your representative. Do not be afraid to ask the questions. You pay for it. And get everything in writing before you sign a contract. The more you ask, the more you know. I highly recommend to get the price from more than one credit card company, so you can decide which salesman tells the truth and who you can put the trust into with one of the most important parts of your business - credit card processing. It is also good to have a spare terminal if your business is busy, for a simple reason. If the one that you are using stops working, you simply connect the other one to the phone line and the problem is solved. Then you call your processor to get the broken terminal fixed. Simple. Saves a lot of time and aggravation. The cost of the terminal is usually around $200 depending on the model. You can buy new Hypercom T7Plus and Nurit 2085 for $220, which is relatively fair. If you need IP connection I suggest OMNI terminals. You should use wireless terminals if you travel for trade shows. Or if you prefer you can buy used one on Ebay, which might save you couple extra dollars, but before you do it, make sure that your processor supports the model that you want to buy.

I recommend that you make sure that you will not have any termination fees, so you can change the processor at any time with no penalty. How can you do that? Just make the salesman call the main office in front of you to make sure that there will be no termination fees.

It won't cost anything to submit the application to the acquirer and termination fee is used only to stop you from leaving. The salesman will do it, believe me. He wants your business. No sale, no money. If the salesman does not want to do that, do not sign anything. Find a different processor. Unfortunately in this industry, there are many dishonest and greedy salespeople who do not tell the truth about the price and mislead the merchants. **Misleading is a crime!** - that's how I view it.

Just consider the damage that untruth may do. Do you like being lied to? These predatory practices make it even more difficult for hardworking salespeople who are honest. Every merchant is entitled to a comprehensive answer. This is my philosophy. An educated merchant means loyal customers. So if you are a merchant, do not rush to sign a deal unless you are one hundred percent sure that this is what you want. Do your research and then make a decision. You are not going to lose a fortune in one month. Even the Bible gives you the advice: "Anyone inexperienced puts faith in every word, but the shrewd one considers his steps" (Proverbs 14:15).

If you are a salesman, be honest. This way you may earn merchant's loyalty for a very long time.

So we already know about the interchange, what to look for in the contract and the processors fees! How exiting that is! Now we'll learn about how the transaction is authorized and what it takes to process it. And that should make it much easier to understand the pricing models used by the processors.

How the transaction is authorized

If you want to understand why you pay all of those fees for the processing of your credit cards, you need to know what this process looks like, and what it takes to make it happen.

Here is how it works: customer swipes the card through the terminal, terminal reads the magnetic stripe, connects with the acquirer's network and submits the request to authorize the transaction.

The acquirer forwards the card and cardholders information to the issuing bank, so the issuer can verify the information and credit available on the card, then sends the authorization code back to the acquirer. After the acquirer receives the authorization code, the transaction is authorized and the merchant can complete the transaction. The process takes about 10 seconds. Unbelievable!

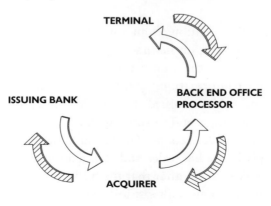

Authorization is used to control credit card fraud. It is the first step in processing the transaction.

The back-end office has access to every transaction that occurs on a daily basis every minute of the day and is responsible for finalizing those transactions and transferring the money to the merchant account. There are thousands of transactions happening every hour! Most merchants are not aware of how many people and how much technology is involved in the entire process. If they did know, it would be easier for them to accept the fact, that they pay for the convenience of accepting electronic payments, which helps them to expand their book of business, simplifies their business operations and increases their revenue.

The acquirer also monitors those transactions to minimize the risk of fraud and to make sure that the cardholders data was not compromised. I understand that it is hard to monitor every merchant and every transaction. There are millions of transactions happening every day and thousands of merchants out there. Who should they monitor? With today's technology, the computer can identify if the card was used twice or three times at the same location or if the card was used in different states moments after the initial use. Obviously, that helps to prevent fraudulent transactions. Merchants can always request the driver's license from the customer to verify his or her identity. I recommend doing that, especially with transactions larger than $500. In any case, the back end office can even hold the funds until the merchant proves that those transactions were valid.

Here's an example: One of my merchants hand-keyed the same credit card number many times and charged it around $4000 each time in one day. The back-end processor can see every transaction at the time of authorization. The transactions were batched out but the back-end office raised a red flag and held the funds until they could verify that those transactions were authorized by the cardholder. They called the merchant the next day and asked if he was committing the fraud. He simply hung up the phone and did not talk to them. It did not help him.

I found out about the situation about a week later. I believe they should have called me, or the cardholder, in the first place. I went to the merchant location and got the invoices from the transactions, a bank statement from the past month and cardholder information; address, phone number etc. I faxed everything to my ISO and told the office staff to call the cardholder to ask, if he authorized those transactions and to verify with the bank that the merchant had a good balance on his bank account. They found out that there was no fraud. The merchant simply had a big order and charged the same corporate card for sixteen different invoices. Soon after that the back-end office released the funds to the merchant bank account. I almost lost a good customer.

Later, I explained everything to the merchant and from that time on, when he has a big transaction or charges the same card multiple times, he calls me one day ahead to let me know about it. This way my ISO and back-end office expect it and do not hold the funds for longer than 48 hours.

Here is another example. Another merchant had two unusual transactions at her location. She owned a deli and did not do any catering. My ISO saw a transaction for $5000 one day, which was very unusual for that merchant. This merchant's average ticket was about $35 and the highest transaction about $120. Red flag! We stopped the funds. We checked the card and found out that it was the owner's credit card. I called her and asked why she used her own card. She simply said, that she did not have enough money to pay the bills and needed fast cash. Can you believe that?

Another time, when she had high ticket transaction, we also checked the card. It came up with different name, so we called the cardholder to ask if he authorized it. He said, that he purchased the goods in this store, so we did not hold the funds. But as you can see, today's technology can discover fraudulent transactions with no problems and the back end office has a team of dedicated people monitoring high risk transactions every hour, every day of the year. Acquirers and processors have enough tools to monitor and stop the fraud before the funds get to the bank account, when it is too late. That is why we have so much technology involved in the entire process.

Recently, Visa and MasterCard introduced new security standards called the PCI Data Security Standard, which is a combination of Visa's Cardholder Information Security Program and MasterCard's Data Protection Program. Can it really help or is it just another fee burden put on the merchant? We will find out shortly. But for now, most of the merchants have to pay the yearly PCI compliant fee.

Let's get now to the pricing plans. We know the interchange and understand the transaction. Now it should be much easier to understand the pricing models used by the processors.

Pricing Plans

Before I talk about the pricing methods used by the Independent Sales Organizations I will share with you some basics. First, lets clarify some merchant banking terminology.

1. *Discount rate* - you see this expression on almost every statement. This is

a percentage of every transaction charged to the merchant. It depends on the type of card used at the merchant location by the customer. Debit cards have the lowest discount rate, credit cards higher. For rewards cards you pay more than for a credit transaction and the merchant pays the most expensive discount rates for business cards, commercial cards and corporate cards.

2. *Transaction fee* - it is a price that you pay for every transaction, every time that a credit or debit card is swiped through the credit card terminal, usually each transaction cost is 0.20 cents.

3. *Batch* - batch contains all the transactions that occurred after the last settlement, after the last close of the day on the credit card terminal.

4. *Settlement* - it is a transmission of all the transactions from the terminal to the acquirer, then the acquirer transmits the money from those transactions to the merchant's bank account. If you will not settle your terminal, you will not see the money on your account. That is why most of the ISO's do automatic batches, so merchants do not have to do the settlement. If you settle your transactions after 72 hours, all of the transactions that were in your terminal downgrade to none qualified rate and cost you more.

With what we have learned in previous chapters, we know enough to understand the language of the merchant banking and its pricing plans. What pricing method is the most transparent?

First and foremost, I recommend the Interchange Past Through pricing plan, which is the best way to buy the product from the credit card company. We know that interchange is non-negotiable, so it makes it easier for us to find out how much we pay for the service, and everything that comes with it. Usually Cost Plus pricing is used for the big guys, I mean the businesses, which have a big monthly processing volume, ranging from about $20,000.00 and up.

I used this pricing method to all of my merchants with no exceptions, with a small mark up, depending on the monthly processing volume, with no termination fees, monthly minimums, annual membership fees and monthly service fees.

I also put in writing that my company will never increase its profit margins for the life of the relationship! This is how I established great relationship with my customers from a very beginning. Not only I have visited their location many times before we signed a deal, but also I was always talking about my offer with the same energy and passion and tried to teach them this business, so they could understand my proposal. When they finally decided to sign a deal with me, they knew, that they had a good deal. They were educated enough about the processing, so they could make a conscious decision before they signed a contract. I had a vision! I knew that merchants would love me for that. I even suggested to my ISO to use only Cost Plus pricing method and assure the merchant that we would never increase our profit. I also recommended that sales people should educate merchants. The more they knew, the more loyal they were to me.

The ISO representative listened carefully and admitted, that this was the best way to price the merchant account, but his office staff was skeptical about the idea saying, that it would make it easier for the competition to steal the account from us. I disagree.

Things changed, after some of his sales reps started to lose many accounts priced differently. He realized that this was the only good pricing plan to keep the merchant from leaving. I realized something from my past experience with sales. You can make good profit only on a volume instead of making money only on one merchant. And I knew that only with Cost Plus the merchant would never leave you. Does this make sense? Make sure that you can get this deal. It is important to get the Cost Plus pricing and not to pay all of these extra fees and be able to cancel your service with no penalty.

Here is an example of what I consider a good deal:

Monthly Processing Volume	Service Fee basis points over Interchange	Percentage that processor makes	Processor's income dollar amount for every $1000
$1.00-$5,000	35-40	0.35%-0.4%	$3.50-$4.00
$5000-$20,000	20-35	0.2%-0.35%	$2.00-$3.50
$20,000-$50,000	15-20	0.15%-0.2%	$1.50-$2.00
$50,000 and up	10 basis - 15 basis	0.1%-0.15%	$1.00-$1.50

All the Cost Plus prices have to come with a 10 cents transaction fee, which is a very fair price. Interchange rates already have another 10 cents so it makes it 20 cents. This way you are buying the product directly from Visa and MasterCard, which is the best way to buy the product, and paying only small percentage and transaction fee for the comfort of having a great local service.

Every ISO out there should be able to offer to you that pricing plan. It is up to you to determine with whom you want to do business. If you do not like the salesman from one company, find another one. No worries. There are plenty of them out there. And everybody wants your business!

Another good price, which is less confusing and many merchants prefer, is Three Tier pricing. But this plan is a bit more complicated and requires an explanation of the terminology.

With that plan all you will see on your statement are only three discount rates, or four if your ISO will give you an extra debit rate:

1. Qualified rate;
2. Mid-qualified rate;
3. None-qualified rate.
4. Debit rate.

What are those rates?

- *Qualified rate* is the discount rate paid for the face-to-face transaction when the card is present and swiped through the magnetic reader. The transaction must be settled within 24 hours otherwise it downgrades to mid-qualified category or none-qualified category.

- *Mid-Qualified rate* is slightly higher than a qualified rate. The transactions that fall into this category are: key-entered transactions with address verifcation service or zip code entered; transactions over the phone, mail or Internet transactions.

- *None-Qualified rate* is what the merchant pays for the rewards cards, business and corporate cards, foreign cards. It is the highest discount rate of all three.

I always gave my merchants a debit rate, which was the lowest from those four so all the debit transactions cost them less than qualified rate. I have to mention that from all the 72 accounts that I opened only four merchants had this pricing plan. Why? They did not understand the Interchange Fees and I was not able to sign a deal using Cost Plus plan. But I always gave them the option to change the pricing plan at any time to different one, if they were not satisfied with Three Tier.

Below is the Three Tier-pricing model that I used for some of my customers:

- Debit rate - 1.39% + .20 cents transaction fee

- Qualified rate - 1.69% + .20 cents transaction fee

- Mid-qualified rate - 2.35% + .20 cents transaction fee

- None-qualified rate - 2.89% + .20 cents transaction fee

This is a very fair price. If you pay much more for the mid-qualified and none-qualified rates now it means that you have a really bad deal. With the rise of the rewards, debit and business cards on the market you should really try to negotiate the best price for those three, because a minority of the transactions will fall into qualified category.

There are also different pricing plans, such as Bill back, Enhanced bill back, Two Tier and Flat rate. Those four plans bring bigger income for the processor, which means that the service price is higher. It depends on the mark up for all the downgrades.

Downgrades are all the transactions from the credit or debit cards that fall into a category different than the qualified rate, which means that it usually is about 50% of all the transactions that take place in your business. As a merchant you should avoid those pricing plans at any cost. All of them come with about 20 cents authorization fees for every transaction. If you pay more than 20 cents, consider renegotiating your price with your current processor. If negotiation will not help, find another processor. You should not even think about getting any pricing plan different than Cost Plus or Three Tier. Also, depending on your average ticket and the volume of debit card transactions, you may benefit from pin-based debit option. Pin based debit transactions usually cost about 50 cents and you can save money on this transaction if your average ticket for debit cards is greater than $50. Then you do not pay any percentage for the transaction, you just pay flat transaction fee around 60 cents. A good way to check the overall percentage that you are paying for the processing of credit card transactions is to divide the fee that you pay by the volume that was processed. If it is greater than 2.7% you should consider finding a new processor.

Here's an example:

On the following statement, the merchant processed an amount of 12,210.55 and was charged a $287.55 fee. Here is how to estimate what percentage you pay for all your transactions:

The monthly processing volume from Visa and MasterCard is only $9415.70. Why is it different than 12,210.55? The amount of $2421.30 was American Express cards and $373.55 was Discover cards. The fee for those cards is paid directly to AMEX and Discover. We always consider only Visa and MasterCard volume including all debit cards.

Amount Deducted:
$ 287.55

Plan Summary

Plan	Number of Sales	Sales Amount	Number of Credits	Credit Amount	Net Sales	Average Ticket	Discount P/I	%	Discount Due
Visa	145	6,488.75	00	.00	6,488.75	44.75	.000	1.490	96.67
MasterCard	72	2,926.95	00	.00	2,926.95	40.65	.000	1.490	43.64
American Express	43	2,421.30	00	.00	2,421.30	56.31	.000	.000	.00
Discover	13	373.55	00	.00	373.55	28.73	.000	.000	.00
Debit	00	.00	00	.00	.00	.00	.000	.000	.00
**	273	12,210.55	00	.00	12,210.55	44.73			140.31

Deposits

Transaction Day	Reference Number	Transaction Description	Plan Description	Number of Sales	Sales Amount	Credit Amount	Discount Paid	Settled
03	90001590010	Deposit	All Card Types	09	538.35	.00	.00	460.05
03	90001600011	Deposit	All Card Types	11	468.90	.00	.00	354.70
03	90001610012	Deposit	All Card Types	12	435.95	.00	.00	363.95
04	90001620016	Deposit	All Card Types	16	478.75	.00	.00	315.20
05	90001630006	Deposit	All Card Types	06	120.85	.00	.00	120.85
06	90001640011	Deposit	All Card Types	11	288.70	.00	.00	153.15
07	90001650006	Deposit	All Card Types	06	145.55	.00	.00	122.55
10	90001660008	Deposit	All Card Types	08	491.80	.00	.00	415.95
10	90001670007	Deposit	All Card Types	07	268.35	.00	.00	148.05
10	90001680014	Deposit	All Card Types	14	925.70	.00	.00	910.70
11	90001690008	Deposit	All Card Types	08	150.90	.00	.00	128.85
12	90001700007	Deposit	All Card Types	07	395.75	.00	.00	175.55
13	90001710007	Deposit	All Card Types	07	503.65	.00	.00	99.75
14	90001720007	Deposit	All Card Types	07	194.35	.00	.00	139.35
17	90001730019	Deposit	All Card Types	18	697.70	.00	.00	650.85
17	90001740001	Deposit	All Card Types	01	61.00	.00	.00	61.00
17	90001750007	Deposit	All Card Types	07	333.40	.00	.00	258.40
17	90001760001	Deposit	All Card Types	01	9.50	.00	.00	9.50
17	90001770007	Deposit	All Card Types	07	313.70	.00	.00	303.65
18	90001780006	Deposit	All Card Types	06	245.75	.00	.00	245.75
19	90001790006	Deposit	All Card Types	06	349.05	.00	.00	289.05
20	90001800014	Deposit	All Card Types	14	388.00	.00	.00	329.25
21	90001810006	Deposit	All Card Types	06	721.90	.00	.00	721.90
24	90001820015	Deposit	All Card Types	15	1,062.40	.00	.00	543.50
24	90001830008	Deposit	All Card Types	08	343.60	.00	.00	232.25
24	90001840001	Deposit	All Card Types	01	38.00	.00	.00	38.00
24	90001850005	Deposit	All Card Types	05	153.50	.00	.00	137.50
26	90001860005	Deposit	All Card Types	05	230.55	.00	.00	230.55
26	90001870008	Deposit	All Card Types	07	335.40	.00	00	209.40
26	90001880001	Deposit	All Card Types	01	60.75	.00	.00	60.75
27	90001890004	Deposit	All Card Types	04	145.80	.00	.00	129.80
27	90001900001	Deposit	All Card Types	01	30.00	.00	.00	30.00
27	90001910001	Deposit	All Card Types	01	18.00	.00	.00	.00
28	90001920004	Deposit	All Card Types	04	100.65	.00	.00	100.65
31	90001930008	Deposit	All Card Types	08	360.50	.00	.00	291.65
31	90001940011	Deposit	All Card Types	11	506.45	.00	.00	336.25
31	90001950006	Deposit	All Card Types	06	217.40	.00	.00	217.40
31	90001960001	Deposit	All Card Types	01	80.00	.00	.00	80.00
Deposit Totals				273	12,210.55	.00	.00	9,415.70

Fees

Number	Amount	Description	Total
16	516.30	MC ENH MID-QUALIFIED	.77
29	1,108.80	MC MID-QUALIFIED	32.35
04	217.85	MASTERCARD NON-QUALIFIED	5.89
03	192.95	MASTERCARD STANDARD	6.80
35	1,450.60	VISA MID-QUALIFIED	39.86
28	2,575.50	VISA NON-QUALIFIED	58.00
02	91.30	VISA STANDARD	3.57
Total Fees Due			147.24

Discount Due	140.31
Fees Due	147.24
Amount Deducted	287.55

QUESTIONS REGARDING YOUR STATEMENT PLEASE CALL 1-800-310-3812.
BE AWARE OF POSSIBLE FRAUD DURING THE HOLIDAY SEASON! FEEL FREE TO CALL US
FOR ANY CONCERNS YOU COULD HAVE REGARDING PROCESSING SUSPICIOUS CARDS.

Merchant pays 1.49% for all the Visa and MasterCard transactions, which looks like a very good deal. We already know, that Interchange Fees for some cards are much higher than 1.49%. How is that this merchant has such a good deal? He does not. Lets analyze that. The statement does not show the cost of a transaction fee so merchant thinks, that his transaction fee is 0. Nice tactic. First, on the bottom of the same page we read that the merchant also pays mid-qualified and none-qualified rates for the cards that did not qualify for the rate of 1.49%. What we do not see is the discount rate that he pays for those downgrades.

The credit card processor simply does not want the merchant to know the real cost, because the merchant would look for another processor if he was aware of those rates. The total charge for processing Visa and MasterCard transactions is $140.31. But what is the cost of the transactions that fell into mid-qualified and none-qualified category? Here is the formula to estimate the discount rate for those transactions:

Number of transactions	Amount processed	Description of the Card	Total Fee	Discount Rate	% paid
16	$ 516.30	MC ENH MID QUAL	$ 0.77	0.001491381	0.15%
29	$1,108.80	MC MID-QUAL	$32.35	0.029175685	2.91%
4	$ 217.85	MC NON-QUAL	$ 5.89	0.027036952	2.70%
3	$ 192.95	MC STANDART	$ 6.80	0.035242291	3.52%
35	$1,450.60	VISA MID-QUAL	$39.86	0.027478285	2.74%
28	$2,575.50	VISA NON-QUAL	$58.00	0.022519899	2.25%
2	$ 91.30	VISA STANDART	$ 3.57	0.039101862	3.91%

Lets add the amounts of the transactions that downgraded to different categories.

Amount
$ 516.30
$1,108.80
$ 217.85
$ 192.95
$1,450.60
$2,575.50
$ 91.30
$6,153.30

So, in addition to the 1.49% that the merchant already paid for $9415.70, $6153.30 fell into different categories and merchant paid additional fee for those transactions, which is listed on a second page of the statement and equals

$147.24. In the last column above we see the percentage paid for the cards that fell into those categories.

Total amount of Visa and MasterCard transactions is $9415.70. If we subtract $6153.30 from 9415.70 we will have the amount of qualified transactions, which is the minority of all the transactions. So, we can see now, that merchant pays additional fees for most of the cards.

Now, we will estimate the overall percentage that merchant pays for the processing. To do that, we need to divide the fees that merchant was charged by the amount that was processed in his location:

Fees	Monthly volume	Percentage paid
287.55	9,415.70	0.030539418

287.55 : 9415.70 = 3.05%

You can apply this formula to every statement out there to find out the overall percentage that the merchant pays for processing his credit card transactions. Of course, not every statement is as easy to read as that one. But I will try to explain how to read the statements in the next chapter using some examples.

I used this method of comparison to most of my potential customers to show them the actual percentage that they pay for the processing. At the same time, I always had 10 statements from my existing clients with me and I applied the same formula for those statements in front of the merchant to show him the difference in price. It always worked. The difference in percentage was usually anywhere between 0.3% to 1.2%. It is easy to understand. It is easier than spreadsheets that we will learn later.

So by consistently using the Cost Plus pricing I built a great relationship with all of my customers and I earned an opinion of an honest businessman.

CHAPTER 3

READING THE STATEMENTS

> "*For wisdom is for a protection [the same as] money is for a protection; but the advantage of knowledge is that wisdom itself preserves alive its owners.*" (Ecclesiastes 7:12).

Here is the fun part. How many of you have problems reading the competition's statements? In the previous chapter I gave you one example of how to read and understand the statements. It was a little introduction to what you'll learn now.

Statements are easy. Once you learn to read them, you can apply your own rates using the spreadsheet on Microsoft Excel. This is another way to show your prospective client the difference between your price and the competition. This technique might be very misleading if you intentionally use the wrong numbers. Dishonest sales people love to mislead. It makes it so much easier to sign the account. I will say it one more time — I personally think that misleading is a crime!

There are many companies out there whose statements are hard to understand. Even their own sales staff sometimes can't understand it. Isn't it funny? Then all you need to do is show the prospect one of your statements and go over it line by line with the merchant. Do not forget to make sure that he understands it. Every merchant loves to know what is on the statement and how to read it. Wouldn't you like to know as well? How many times have you heard the expression: I don't know what I am paying for! Well, now you will be able to answer the merchant's question.

If you can teach merchants this simple thing — reading and understanding the statements — it will help you to close a deal. Take the statement home and make the comparison. Here you will find some of the statements and spreadsheets that I had the pleasure to work on in the past. I hope it will help you to understand the process of comparing the rates much better. If you know how to read the statement and you understand it, you are already half way to sign a deal. All you need to do is to set up another appointment, prepare your speech and go over the numbers with the merchant. Did I say be prepared? Always be prepared.

After 30 statements you won't have to do the spreadsheet anymore. I always do it, because it is easier for the merchant to digest all the information. It's easy. You will master it and be able to write the difference in price right away. It takes only five minutes, although some of the statements are more complicated, like the enhanced bill back. Not to worry — you will learn that one too. Just make sure that the numbers are accurate. This way, when the merchant received your first statement, you will be able to sleep well. Otherwise you will be getting a lot of unhappy phone calls - and that's if you are lucky. Some of the merchants will not even call you. They'll simply go back to a previous processor or find another one. But if they do call you, you'd better pick up the phone. If you don't answer those calls, you can be sure that your hard work to sign the merchant was nothing more than a waste of time. The merchant will leave you and your company. A good salesman always tells the truth and answers the phone. Why? Because he knows he has done nothing wrong and is willing to explain the contract one more time and help the merchant to understand the statement. Only salespeople who lie do not answer the phone. They simply do not want to talk to the angry merchant. They figure that the merchant will calm down after a month. It will be too much of a hassle for the merchant to find another processor, so the salesman can benefit from the account untill this happens. Plus the high termination fee might prevent the merchant from switching again.

Remember - not every phone call from the merchant means the bad news. Sometimes the merchant might call you with a referral. That is another good reason to always pick up the phone.

Now, I'll go over some statements.

Here is the first example of how to read and compare the rates:

$ 94.07
AMOUNT DEDUCTED FROM ACCOUNT

PLAN SUMMARY

PL	# SALES	$ SALES	# CREDITS	$ CREDITS	NET SALES	AVG TKT	DISC P/I	%	DISCOUNT DUE
V	86	3,168.36	00	.00	3,168.36	36.84	.000	1.610	50.99
VD	41	1,638.45	00	.00	1,638.45	39.96	.000	1.610	26.35
VB	00	.00	00	.00	.00		.000	1.610	.00
M	43	1,472.99	00	.00	1,472.99	34.26	.000	1.610	23.70
MD	19	974.30	00	.00	974.30	51.28	.000	1.610	15.69
MB	00	.00	00	.00	.00		.000	1.610	.00
P2	00	.00	00	.00	.00		.000	.000	.00
VA	00	.00	00	.00	.00		.000	1.610	.00
MA	00	.00	00	.00	.00		.000	1.610	.00
VL	00	.00	00	.00	.00		.000	1.610	.00
ML	00	.00	00	.00	.00		.000	1.610	.00
DB	190	2,031.23	00	.00	2,031.23	10.69	.000	.000	.00
**	379	9,285.33	00	.00	9,285.33	24.50			116.73

DAY	REF NUMBER	*	PL	# SALES	$ SALES	$ CREDITS	DISCOUNT PD	SETTLED
				DEPOSITS				
01	40242001000	D	VD	02	105.50	.00		.00
01	40242001000	D	V	03	98.37	.00		.00
01	40242001000	D	M	03	106.52	.00		.00
01	40242001000	D	DB	08	75.96	.00	8.98	377.37
01	40243001000	D	V	04	207.18	.00		.00
01	40243001000	D	MD	01	35.10	.00		.00
01	40243001000	D	M	02	89.26	.00		.00
01	40243001000	D	DB	06	97.65	.00	9.74	419.45
01	40244001000	D	V	01	31.31	.00		.00
01	40244001000	D	M	01	21.89	.00		.00
01	40244001000	D	DB	05	53.38	.00	1.39	105.19
02	40245001000	D	VD	02	164.10	.00		.00
02	40245001000	D	V	03	97.04	.00		.00
02	40245001000	D	M	01	47.94	.00		.00
02	40245001000	D	DB	04	33.82	.00	6.04	336.86
03	40246001000	D	V	01	24.22	.00		.00
03	40246001000	D	DB	03	19.77	.00	.98	43.01
04	40247001000	D	V	03	91.98	.00		.00

PL (PLAN CODES)
V - VISA   P - PRIVATE LABEL   T - ALL PLANS   2 - PLAN TWO   A - CASH ADVANCES   D - DEBIT CARD
M - MASTERCARD   L - LARGE TICKET   1 - PLAN ONE   3 - PLAN THREE   B - BUSINESS CARD

* (TRANSACTION CODES)
D - DEPOSIT   A - ADJUSTMENT
C - CHARGEBACK   B - CHARGEBACK REVERSAL

Let's start from the very top right corner. According to the information provided here, the amount deducted from merchant account should be $94.07. But is it accurate? Is this really the amount that merchant paid for the processing of $9,285.33? If yes, it would be the best price the merchant could get, price way below the interchange that processor pays to card brands, lower than the actual cost of the cards processed at the location. Let's analyze it a bit closer.

$94.07 : $9,285.33 = 1.01% It looks like an unbelievably great deal!

But take a closer look at the bottom left corner of the first column and you will see that the amount of $2,031.23 represents debit cards where the merchant does not pay any percentage except transaction fee, which we do not see at all at the first page. So the total amount of credit card processed is $9,285.33 - $2,031.23 = $7,254.1 Are you still following me?

```
                                                            $   94.07
                                           AMOUNT DEDUCTED FROM ACCOUNT
                          FEES
NUMBER      AMOUNT     DESCRIPTION                                TOTAL
------      ------     -----------                                -----
   37      1,467.74    1 VISA CPS REWARDS 1                       33.35
   04        109.58    2 MASTERCARD WORLD CONV PURCHASE             2.64
   01         72.47    1 MASTERCARD ENHANCED MERIT 3                1.56
   28        896.72    1 MASTERCARD ENHANCED CONV PURCHASE         20.91
   01         24.97    3 MC INTERNATIONAL SALE ASSESSMENT FEE        .17
   02         46.69    1 MASTERCARD CONVENIENCE                     1.14
   02         86.54    1 MASTERCARD WORLD MERIT 3                   1.95
   01         26.92    INTERLINK DEBIT NETWORK FEES                  .33
   32                  BATCH HEADER FEE @ $0.25 EACH                8.00
                       STATEMENT FEE                               10.00
  193                  TRANSACTION FEE 0.200 EACH                  38.60
   01                  DEBIT TRANSACTION FEE 0.25 EACH               .25
  205                  EBT TRANSACTION FEE 0.18 EACH               36.90
                                               TOTAL FEES DUE     155.80

                    DISCOUNT DUE      116.73
                    DISCOUNT PAID     116.73
                    FEES DUE          155.80
                    FEES PAID          61.73
                    NET FEES DUE       94.07
                    AMOUNT DEDUCTED    94.07
```

EFFECTIVE OCTOBER 1, 2008, VISA AND MASTERCARD WILL MAKE CHANGES TO
PRICING FOR SOME OF THEIR INTERCHANGE CLASSES. DUE TO THIS, YOU MAY SEE
SLIGHTLY INCREASED FEES FOR YOUR PROCESSING AS OF THAT DATE.
WE STRIVE TO KEEP YOUR COSTS AS LOW AS POSSIBLE WHILE CONTINUNING TO
PROVIDE YOU WITH SERVICE EXCELLENCE.
WE THANK YOU FOR YOUR CONTINUED PATRONAGE!
FOR QUESTIONS REGARDING YOUR STATEMENT, PLEASE CALL US AT 866-201-1100 FOR
24/7 TECHNICAL SUPPORT, PLEASE CALL THE NUMBER ON YOUR TERMINAL STICKER.

IN ASSOCIATION WITH BANK OF AMERICA, N.A., CHARLOTTE, NC

```
                        PL (PLAN CODES)                                      * (TRANSACTION CODES)
V - VISA        P - PRIVATE LABEL  T - ALL PLANS  2 - PLAN TWO    A - CASH ADVANCES   D - DEBIT CARD    D - DEPOSIT       A - ADJUSTMENT
M - MASTERCARD  L - LARGE TICKET   1 - PLAN ONE   3 - PLAN THREE  B - BUSINESS CARD                     C - CHARGEBACK    B - CHARGEBACK REVERSAL
```

Let's look now at the percentage that the merchant is being charged for all the cards. The percentage stated here equals to 1.61% for every single type of the card: Visa -V, Visa Debit - VD, Visa Business - VB, MasterCard - M, MasterCard Debit - MD.

We do not see any transaction fees, only the discount rate. But we know the interchange now, don't we? We know that different cards have different discount rates and also a transaction fee, plus the acquirer charges an extra 0.6 cents for the authorization. What is wrong with the picture?

For all the cards that were processed, the merchant was charged $116.73, which is stated on the same page. Why then does the statement say that the amount deducted from the merchant account was only $94.07? Simply, because the processor is hiding something. Lets add $116.73 to $94.07 and then we may get a little closer to the actual processing cost of those transactions.

$116.73 + $94.07 = $210.80

To accurately estimate the percentage that the merchant pays just on the first page we need to divide the added number by the amount of credit card processed excluding debit amount $9,285.33 - $2,031.23 = $7,254.1.

Then we have the number:

$116.73 + $94.07 = $210.80 : $7,254.1 = 2.90%

This looks more like it. But we are not quite there yet. Let's look at the last page of this statement. Here, we will find the last piece of this puzzle. The last page shows us the interchange categories that the merchant had to pay for, and the breakdown of those categories with the amount processed for all of them.

Number of transactions	Amount	Description	Fees	Cost of processing	Actual percentage
37	$1,467.74	1 Visa CPS Rewards 1	$33.35	0.022722008	2.27%
4	$ 109.58	2 MasterCard World conv Purchase	$ 2.64	0.024091988	2.41%
1	$ 72.47	1 MasterCard Enhanced Merit 3	$ 1.56	0.021526149	2.15%
28	$ 896.72	1 MasterCard Enhanced Conv Purchase	$20.91	0.023318316	2.33%
1	$ 24.97	3 MC International Sale Assessment Fee	$ 0.17	0.00680817	0.68%
2	$ 46.69	1 MasterCard Convinience	$ 1.14	0.024416363	2.44%
2	$ 86.64	1 MasterCard World Merit 3	$ 1.95	0.022506925	2.25%
1	$ 26.92	Interlink Debit Network Fees	$ 0.33	0.012258544	1.22%
32		Batch	$ 8.00		
		Statement	$ 10.00		
193		Transaction Fee	$ 38.60		
1		Debit Transaction Fee	$ 0.25		
205		EBT Transaction Fee	$ 36.90		
		Total Fees	$155.80		

Now we can analyze it accurately. We know that the merchant already paid 1.61% for all the transactions on the first page. All we need to do is to add this discount rate to the interchange categories, which are listed on the last page. So the final discount rate for Rewards cards that the merchant paid is 2.27% + 1.61% = 3.88% Wow!!!

We can apply this formula to the rest of the categories. So what is the final bill? Why is it so confusing? We can read it in the last column.

Discount Due	116.73
Discount Paid	116.73
Fees Due	155.80
Fees Paid	61.73
Net Fees Due	94.07
Amount Deducted	94.07

This is the last analysis. From that column we will get the final figure. Discount Due - Discount Paid $116.73 was deducted at the same day that the transactions took place. The processor simply charged the merchant for the transactions 1.61% at the time of the settlement. Fees Due - Fees Paid $61.73 were charged at the same time, the time of the settlement and represent the fees for all the interchange categories from the last page minus the Net Fees Due $155.80 - $94.07 = $61.73.

Description	Fees
1 Visa CPS Rewards 1	$33.35
2 MasterCard World Conv Purchase	$ 2.64
1 MasterCard Enhanced Merit 3	$ .56
1 MasterCard Enhanced Conv Purchase	$20.91
3 MC International Sale Assessment Fee	$ 0.17
1 MasterCard Convinience	$ 1.14
1 MasterCard World Merit 3	$ 1.95
Interlink Debit Network Fees	$ 0.33
Total Fees	$61.73

All we have left are Net Fees due that were deducted at the end of the month - $94.07 So total amount that the merchant paid for the processing is $116.73 + $94.07 + 61.73 = $272.53

And it includes all credit and debit card processing fees, batch fees, statement fee, settlement and transaction fees. This way, we can find out what overall percentage the merchant pays for the processing:

$272.53 : $9,285.33 = 2.93%

Let's see, how much money we can save this merchant a month by applying our pricing plans and discount rates. Let's use, for example the cost-plus plan with mark up of 0.3% and 20 cents transaction fee.

Here is the first spreadsheet for you:

Processor	Volume	Discount Rate	Item Count	Item Rate	Fees
Visa	$3,168.36	0.0161	86		$ 51.01
Visa Debit	$1,638.45	0.0161	41		$ 26.38
Visa Business	-	0.0161	0		-
MasterCard	$1,472.99	0.0161	43		$ 23.72
MasterCard Debit	$ 974.30	0.0161	19		$ 15.69
MasterCard Business	-	0.0161	0		-
Debit	$2,031.23		190		-
Visa CPS Rewards	$1,467.74	0.0227	37		$ 33.32
MC World Conv Purch	$ 109.58	0.0241	4		$ 2.64
MC Enhanced Merit 3	$ 72.47	0.0215	1		$ 1.56
MC Enhanced Conv Purch	$ 896.72	0.0233	28		$ 20.89
MC International Sale Ass	$ 24.97	0.0068	1		$ 0.17
MC Convinience	$ 46.69	0.0244	2		$ 1.14
MC World Merit 3	$ 86.54	0.0225	2		$ 1.95
Interlink Debit Network Fee	$ 26.92	0.0122	1		$ 0.33
Batch			32	$ 0.25	$ 8.00
Statement Fee			1	$10.00	$ 10.00
Transaction Fee			193	$ 0.20	$ 38.60
Debit Transaction Fee			1	$ 0.25	$ 0.25
EBT Transaction Fee			205	$ 0.18	$ 36.90
Total Fees					$272.54

This spreadsheet shows the fees that the merchant pays to the current processor. Now, we will make another one, but this time we will apply our discount rates and compare the savings.

You	Volume	Discount Rate	Item Count	Item Rate	Fees
Visa	$3,168.36	0.003	86		$ 9.51
Visa Debit	$1,638.45	0.0133	41		$ 21.79
Visa Business	-	0	0		-
MasterCard	$1,472.99	0.003	43		$ 4.42
MasterCard Debit	$ 974.30	0.0135	19		$ 13.15
MasterCard Business	-	0.003	0		-
Debit	$2,031.23		190		-
Visa CPS Rewards	$1,467.74	0.0165	37		$ 24.22
MC World Conv Purch	$ 109.58	0.02	4		$ 2.19
MC Enhanced Merit 3	$ 72.47	0.0215	1		$ 1.56
MC Enhanced Conv Purch	$ 896.72	0.019	28		$ 17.04
MC International Sale Ass	$ 24.97	0.003	1		$ 0.07
MC Convinience	$ 46.69	0.019	2		$ 0.89
MC World Merit 3	$ 86.54	0.0173	2		$ 1.50
Interlink Debit Network Fee	$ 26.92	0.0122	1		$ 0.33
Batch			32	$0.15	$ 4.80
Statement Fee			1	$8.50	$ 8.50
Transaction Fee			193	$0.20	$ 38.60
Debit Transaction Fee			1	$0.25	$ 0.25
EBT Transaction Fee			205	$0.18	$ 36.90
MasterCard	$ 236.02	0.0158			$ 3.73
Visa	$1,700.62	0.0154			$ 26.19
Visa Assessment	$4,806.81	0.000925			$ 4.45
MasterCard Assessment	$2,447.29	0.00095			$ 2.32
Total Fees					$222.40
Monthly Savings					$ 50.13
Annual Savings					$601.62

What we have done here is simply applied the interchange fees for all the cards plus assessments and marked up 0.3% as our profit margins. If you look at the spreadsheet, you will see debit interchange fees already marked up from 1.03% for Visa to 1.33% and MasterCard from 1.05% to 1.35%.

On the bottom of this spreadsheet you will see volume, which you do not see on the statement and discount rates right next to it. What are they? These amounts represent transactions, which did not downgrade to higher interchange categories.

How did I come up with those amounts? If you look closely at the statement, you will see that the merchant paid 1.61% for all the transactions. He also paid additional discount rate for the cards that fell into other categories. The amounts that you see are the differences between the interchange categories and total amount processed:

$3,168.36 (all visa cards except debit) - $1,467.74 (Visa Rewards 1 - downgrade) = $1,700.62 - this number represents Visa CPS Retail category, which cost 1.54%.

How do I know that? It did not downgrade to any other category and we can see debit cards charged separately.

It is the same scenario with MasterCard. All the downgrades round up to:

MC World Conv Purch	$ 109.58
MC Enhanced Merit 3	$ 72.47
MC Enhanced Conv Purch	$ 896.72
MC International Sale Ass	$ 24.97
MC Convinience	$ 46.69
MC World Merit 3	$ 86.54
Total	**$1,236.97**

And we have our MC domestic Merit 3 - $1,472.99 - $1,236.97 = $236.02

As you can see, this merchant was paying a fortune for processing only $9,285.33. Monthly savings are $50.13. Add to it the annual fees that this merchant pays, and you just saved him over $601.56 a year on credit card processing. Just imagine how much money you can save somebody who has the same pricing plan but his monthly processing volume is $50,000!

- INFORMATION ONLY -

```
*------------------------------- DEPOSITS --------------------------------*
DAY   REF NO.      ITEMS  $---- SALES ---$  $ CREDITS$  $- DISC -$  $  NET DEPOSIT $
01  98793331405     11          624.99          .00         .00            624.99
05  98794648215     25        1,291.99          .00         .00          1,291.99
05  98795788594     25        2,453.41          .00         .00          2,453.41
05  98796495379     18        1,372.95          .00         .00          1,372.95
05  98797108078     25        1,948.65          .00         .00          1,948.65
06  98798048613     21        1,423.24          .00         .00          1,423.24
07  98799144836     16        1,285.95          .90         .00          1,285.95
08  98790248364     14          686.09          .00         .00            686.09
11  98791496256     14        1,195.98          .00         .00          1,195.98
11  98792613739     25        1,991.45          .00         .00          1,991.45
11  98793295350      5          316.98          .00         .00            316.98
12  98794200199      8          976.99          .00         .00            976.99
13  98795229299      9          499.96        10.00         .00            489.96
14  98796279362      5          132.00          .00         .00            132.00
15  98797341776     15          973.57          .00         .00            973.57
18  98798630978     23        1,561.46       105.01         .00          1,456.45
18  98799801223     19        1,822.85       131.00         .00          1,691.85
18  98790514481      8          365.71          .00         .00            365.71
19  98791421374      8          744.47          .00         .00            744.47
20  98792478458     10          595.96          .00         .00            595.96
21  98793543732      6          501.99          .00         .00            501.99
22  98794627780      6          462.00          .00         .00            462.00
25  98795868137     28        1,761.40        35.99         .00          1,725.41
25  98796987375     31        1,949.94        77.98         .00          1,871.96
25  98797680642      6          523.99          .00         .00            523.99
26  98798565843     11          823.99          .00         .00            823.99
27  98799635611     13          881.98          .00         .00            881.98
28  98790673361      9          410.48          .00         .00            410.48
29  98791756361     20        1,297.34          .00         .00          1,297.34

DEPOSIT TOTALS:    29       30,877.76       359.98         .00         30,517.78

                 *--------* DEPOSIT ITEM SUMMARY *--------*
   SALES   :    428       30,877.76    DB ADJ :        0               .00
   CREDITS:      6           359.98    CR ADJ :        0               .00
   TOTAL   :    434       30,517.78    TOTAL  :        0               .00
```

Does this make sense? We can also break it down for qualified, mid-qualified and non-qualified categories but it takes much more time, because you need to find out which transactions fall into those categories. Just remember to always have the interchange fee schedule with you, so you can show these fees to the merchant.

Let's move to the next statement.

This pricing plan is very similar to the previous one. But lets practice reading the statements and the spreadsheets. This way you may gain better understanding of what we do here.

This statement says that the merchant account was debited $696.53. And the number is accurate. Why is it accurate? Simply because it is a different pricing model, different processor, and discounts rates are not too high.

```
                    *- INFORMATION ONLY  -*

            *--------* SETTLEMENT/DISCOUNT  *--------*
                                               DISC     ITEM
*-------* DESCRIPTION *------*  ITEMS  $--- AMOUNT ---$  AVG TICKET  RATE    RATE     FEE AMOUNT
VISA                              43     2,892.67         67.27    1.8100   .2250      62.04
-VIBS                             11       811.99         73.82    1.7000   .2250      16.28
VDBT  EIRF                        10       681.21         68.12    1.6600   .2750      14.06
VDBT  CPS                        300    21,252.40         70.84    1.6600   .2750     435.30
VDBT  REF                          5          .00           .00    1.6600   .2250       1.13
MC    M-3                         39     2,942.61         75.45    1.9000   .2250      64.69
MC    KEYD                         1       120.00        120.00    1.9000   .2250       2.51
MC    REF                          1          .00           .00    1.8100   .2250        .23
MC    WCRD                         1        40.00         40.00    1.9000   .2250        .99
MDBT                              23     2,136.88         92.91    1.7400   .2750      43.51
TOTAL                                                                                  640.74

                *----------*   SURCHARGES   *---------*
                                ITEMS    $--- AMOUNT ---$         FEE AMOUNT
NQS-VS KEY ENTERED                11          865.20                13.15
NQS-VS REWARDS 1                  12          811.00                 2.43
NQS-VS CORP CARD                  11          811.99                12.34
NQS-VS KEY ENTERED                 7          384.99                 4.31
NQS-MC KEY ENTERED                 1          120.00                 1.34
NQS-MC WORLD CARD MERIT 3          1           40.00                 0.12
TOTAL                                                               33.69

                *----------*   OTHER FEES   *---------*
CARD CHARGE DESCRIPTION          NUMBER          RATE              FEES
FOR OUTLET 00000
AMEX 2900    AMEX PER ITEM         17           .1000              1.70
DISC 2902    DISCOVER PER ITEM      4           .1000               .40
     6003    SRVICE FEE             0           .0000             10.00
     6128    NDPS FEE               0           .0000             10.00
                        TOTAL OTHER FEES :                         22.10

            YOUR ACCOUNT HAS BEEN DEBITED :                       696.53
```

If we apply our formula here, we can see that the merchant pays 2.25% for the processing. Good deal. Is there anything we can do for this guy? Yes. Let's analyze it.

On the top of the first page we can see the discount rates for all different categories of the cards processed at this location. When we look lower at the statement, we see surcharges for the cards that fell into the non-qualified category. And finally, on the bottom of the statement we can read fees for service and transactions. There is something else here. Do you see the amount 0.00 for VDBT REF, which shows 5 transactions, no volume and a charge of $1.13? And MC REF, one transaction, also 0.00 volume and fee of $0.23? If you will look at the last page, you will see that this merchant had six refunds. This explains no volume for those cards, and fee being charged just for the authorizations.

So what can we do to save this merchant some money and to also make some?

Let's figure out first the discount rates for non-qualified transactions:

Item count	Amount	Description	Fees	Cost of processing	Discount Rate %
11	$865.20	NQS-VS Key Entered	$13.15	0.015198798	1.51%
12	$811.00	NQS-VS Rewards 1	$ 2.43	0.002996301	0.30%
11	$811.99	NQS-VS Corp Card	$12.34	0.015197231	1.51%
7	$384.99	NQS-VS Key Entered	$ 4.31	0.011195096	1.12%
1	$120.00	NQS-MC Key Entered	$ 1.34	0.011166667	1.12%
1	$ 40.00	NQS-MC Wrld Merit 3	$ 0.12	0.003	0.30%

Now we know, what rates we should apply in our spreadsheet.

Here is how we do it:

Processor	Volume	Discount Rate	Item Count	Item Rate	Fees
Visa	$ 2,892.67	0.0181	43	$ 0.23	$ 62.03
Visa Business	$ 811.99	0.017	11	$ 0.23	$ 16.28
Visa Debit EIRF	$ 681.21	0.0166	10	$ 0.28	$ 14.06
Visa Debit CPS	$21,252.40	0.0166	300	$ 0.28	$435.29
Visa Debit REF	-	0.0166	5	$ 0.23	$ 1.13
MC Merit 3	$ 2,942.61	0.019	39	$ 0.23	$ 64.68
MC KEYD	$ 120.00	0.019	1	$ 0.23	$ 2.51
MC REF	-	0.0181	1	$ 0.23	$ 0.23
MC WCRD	$ 40.00	0.019	1	$ 0.23	$ 0.99
MC Debit	$ 2,136.88	0.0174	23	$ 0.28	$ 43.51
None-Qualif VS Key Entered	$ 865.20	0.0151	11		$ 3.06
None-Qualif VS Rewards 1	$ 811.00	0.003	12		$ 2.43
None-Qualif VS Corp Card	$ 811.99	0.0151	11		$ 12.26
None-Qualif VS Key Entered	$ 384.99	0.0112	7		$ 4.31
None-Qualif MC Key Entered	$ 120.00	0.0112	1		$ 1.34
None-Qualif MC Wrld Merit 3	$ 40.00	0.003	1		$ 0.12
AMEX			17	$ 0.10	$ 1.70
DISCOVER			4	$ 0.10	$ 0.40
Service Fee			1	$10.00	$ 10.00
NDPS Fee			1	$10.00	$ 10.00
Total					$696.32

If you compare the fees that the merchant paid, the spreadsheet shows exactly the same amount and discount rates. Below are our discount rates.

You	Volume	Discount Rate	Item Count	Item Rate	Fees
Visa	$ 2,892.67	0.0169	43	$0.20	$ 57.49
Visa Business	$ 811.99	0.0289	11	$0.20	$ 25.67
Visa Debit EIRF	$ 681.21	0.0229	10	$0.20	$ 17.60
Visa Debit CPS	$21,252.40	0.013	300	$0.20	$ 336.28
Visa Debit REF	-	0.0229	5	$0.20	$ 1.00
MC Merit 3	$ 2,942.61	0.0175	39	$0.20	$ 59.30
MC KEYD	$ 120.00	0.0289	1	$0.20	$3.67
MC REF	-	0.0289	1	$0.20	$0.20
MC WCRD	$ 40.00	0.0289	1	$0.20	$1.36
MC Debit	$ 2,136.88	0.013	23	$0.20	$ 32.38
None-Qualif VS Key Entered	$ 865.20	0	11	-	-
None-Qualif VS Rewards 1	$ 811.00	0	12	-	-
None-Qualif VS Corp Card	$ 811.99	0	11	-	-
None-Qualif VS Key Entered	$ 384.99	0	7	-	-
None-Qualif MC Key Entered	$ 120.00	0	1	-	-
None-Qualif MC Wrld Merit 3	$ 40.00	0	1	-	-
AMEX			17	$0.10	$ 1.70
DISCOVER			4	$0.10	$ 0.40
Service Fee			1	$8.50	$ 8.50
NDPS Fee			1	-	-
Visa Assesment Fee	$25,638.27	0.000925			$ 23.72
MC Assesment Fee	$ 5,239.49	0.00095			$ 4.98
Batch			30	$0.10	$ 3.00
Total					$ 577.23
Monthly Savings					$ 119.30
Annual Savings					$1,431.60

The changes I made to this pricing plan are as follows:

I decided not to charge extra rates for the cards that fall into the non-qualified category. Instead, I raised the price for those cards from 1.81% and 1.90% to 2.89%. This way, the merchant can save some money on those transactions. But the biggest savings come from debit cards. Previously, the merchant paid 1.66%. We know that interchange fee for debit card is 1.03% for Visa and 1.05% for MasterCard. I lowered those two discount rates to 1.3%. The majority of the transactions at this location fell into debit category, totaling 323 transactions and the volume of $23,389.28. This way I saved the merchant the most money on debit cards, and still make money on those cards! 1.3%-1.03% = 0.27% profit margins.

I also added assessment fees and batch fees to be more accurate. I estimated that the merchant should have 30 batches a month and applied this fee to my spreadsheet. If you will look at the processor's statement and spreadsheet, these fees are not being charged. Remember. Always try to be as accurate as possible and add to your spreadsheet every fee that you are going to charge your prospect.

According to the pricing plan, my income just from debit cards will be $63.15.

0.27% x ($21,252.40 + $2,136.88) = $63.15
     (Visa Debit) (MasterCard Debit)

Even if I lose some small amount of money on business cards, I will be able to have a decent income from this account. And it will be hard to beat the price. I also waived the NDPS fee.

The pricing plan used here is three tier with the following rates:
Visa Qualified rate - 1.69% + .20 cents
MasterCard Qualified rate - 1.75% + .20 cents
Mid-Qualified rate - 2.29% + .20 cents
None-Qualified rate - 2.89% + .20 cents
Debit rate - 1.3% + .20 cents

So, what is the overall percentage that the merchant is paying now?

$577.23 : 30,877.76 = 1.86%

The percentage is low, because the majority of the transactions fall into debit category. If the location has more business cards and commercial cards this number will be much higher.

So, merchant saved again almost $120.00 a month.

Now, I will show you a statement with cost plus pricing. This one might be tricky. Why? Just look at it, and think. On this statement it looks like the merchant pays just a cost price. How is it possible? Nobody can get those deals! The processor would not make any money! Let's use our formula and divide the fees that merchant paid by the volume that was processed for Visa and MasterCard transactions.

Credit Card Summary

Card	Number Of Items	Sales	Number Of Items	Credits	Total Number Of Items	Net Sales	Average Ticket
MASTERCARD	326	$ 4,085.86	0	$ 0.00	326	$ 4,085.86	$ 12.53
VISA	399	$ 4,746.26	0	$ 0.00	399	$ 4,746.26	$ 11.90
DISCOVER	0	$ 0.00	0	$ 0.00	0	$ 0.00	$ 0.00
DINERS CLUB	0	$ 0.00	0	$ 0.00	0	$ 0.00	$ 0.00
AMERICAN EXPRESS	146	$ 3,255.46	0	$ 0.00	146	$ 3,255.46	$ 22.30
Totals	871	$ 12,087.58	0	$ 0.00	871	$ 12,087.58	

Charges & Fees

Description		Sales Amount	Items	Rate	Item Charge	Amount Charged*
MasterCard Charges:	MC COMMERCIAL T&E I (US) CORP	$ 34.74	3	2.35%		$ 0.82
	MC COMMERCIAL T&EI (US) BUSINESS	$ 160.37	14	2.35%		$ 3.76
	MC DOMESTIC MERIT III (DB)	$ 135.39	3	1.05%	$ 0.15	$ 1.87
	MC DOMESTIC MERIT III	$ 208.34	18	1.58%	$ 0.10	$ 5.10
	MC ENHANCED KEY ENTERED	$ 409.35	7	2.04%	$ 0.10	$ 9.05
	MC ENHANCED MERIT III BASE	$ 353.00	36	1.73%	$ 0.10	$ 9.70
	MC FOREIGN ELECTRONIC PLUS (US LOCATIONS)	$ 25.66	2	1.61%		$ 0.41
	MC FOREIGN STANDARD PLUS (US LOCATIONS)	$ 4.41	1	2.14%	$ 0.10	$ 0.19
	MC KEY ENTERED	$ 25.00	1	1.89%	$ 0.10	$ 0.57
	MC KEY ENTERED DEBIT	$ 228.34	14	1.64%	$ 0.16	$ 5.98
	MC RESTAURANT DEBIT	$ 683.31	34	1.19%	$ 0.10	$ 11.52
	MC SMALL TICKET DEBIT	$ 1,319.53	152	1.55%	$ 0.04	$ 26.52
	MC WORLD RESTAURANT	$ 285.60	25	1.73%	$ 0.10	$ 7.44
	MC WRLD ELITE OTHER	$ 47.75	2	2.75%	$ 0.10	$ 1.51
	MC WRLD ELITE RESTAURANT	$ 122.12	12	1.73%	$ 0.10	$ 3.32
	MC WRLD T&E (DINING/TRAVEL AGENT)	$ 42.95	2	2.30%	$ 0.10	$ 1.19
Total MasterCard Sales Fees						$ 88.97
Visa Charges:	VS CPS BUSINESS CARD T&E	$ 212.45	17	2.40%	$ 0.10	$ 6.81
	VS CPS SMALL TICKET PROGRAM	$ 607.77	69	1.65%	$ 0.04	$ 12.78
	VS CPS/RESTAURANT CREDIT	$ 256.67	6	1.54%	$ 0.10	$ 4.55
	VS CPS/RESTAURANT DEBIT	$ 1,037.13	51	1.19%	$ 0.10	$ 17.45
	VS CPS/REWARD 2	$ 186.94	9	1.90%	$ 0.10	$ 4.45
	VS CPS/SMALL TICKET DEBIT	$ 1,914.01	218	1.55%	$ 0.04	$ 38.40
	VS EIRF DEBIT	$ 313.50	17	1.75%	$ 0.20	$ 8.89
	VS EIRF NON-CPS - ALL OTHER	$ 73.25	3	2.30%	$ 0.10	$ 1.98
	VS SIGNATURE CARD ELECTRONIC	$ 109.97	6	2.30%	$ 0.10	$ 3.12
	VS SIGNATURE CARD STANDARD	$ 17.61	1	2.70%	$ 0.10	$ 0.58
	VS SIGNATURE PREFERRED - ELECTRONIC T&E	$ 16.96	2	2.30%	$ 0.10	$ 0.59

*Calculated daily, rounding differences may occur

†Bank account number ********1865
†Reflects most current bank account number
**Chargeback Interchange Refund
***Chargeback Reversal Interchange Expense

$400.93 : $8,832.12 = 4.53%

Unbelievable! The merchant pays more than 4.5%! How is that? Did you find the trick that the salesman used?

Here is the trick:

Charges & Fees

Description		Sales Amount	Items	Rate	Item Charge	Amount Charged*
	Total Visa Sales Fees					$ 99.60
Auth Fees:	MASTERCARD WATS AUTH FEE		329		$ 0.20	$ 65.80
	VISA WATS AUTH FEE		404		$ 0.20	$ 80.80
	AMEX WATS AUTH FEE		149		$ 0.25	$ 37.25
	Total Auth Fees		882			$ 183.85
Other Fees:	BATCH SETTLEMENT FEE		31		$ 0.25	$ 7.75
	VISA INTL SERVICE FEE		7			$ 0.44
	MASTERCARD ASSESSMENT FEE	$ 4,085.86		0.095%		$ 3.88
	VISA ASSESSMENT FEE	$ 4,746.26		0.0925%		$ 4.40
	MMV MONTHLY ACCESS FEE					$ 1.95
	MONTHLY STATEMENT FEE					$ 10.00
	US CROSS BORDER FEE		2			$ 0.09
	Total of Other Fees	$ 8,832.12	40			$ 28.51
Total Charges and Fees						$ 400.93

Look at the last page. Most of the transactions at this location are below $15.00, which is considered as a small ticket transaction. The interchange transaction fee for small ticket is 1.55% + .04 cents. If you look closely, you will see that this merchant pays an extra 20 cents for every authorization on the top of interchange transaction fee, which together equals 30 cents for credit cards, 35 cents for debit cards and 24 cents for small ticket transactions. We know that the average ticket for most of the transactions here is about $12.00. If we divide: 20 cents : $12.00 = 1.66% that the merchant pays right away not including discount rates.

So all we need to do here is to lower the transaction fee to 10 cents and mark up all interchange categories by 0.2% to make some money.

Let's find out how much money we can save this merchant based on this spreadsheet:

First comes the processor's spreadsheet:

Processor	Volume	Discount Rate	Item Count	Item Rate	Fees
MC COMMERCIAL T&E US CORP	$ 34.74	0.0235	3	-	$ 0.82
MC COMMERCIAL T&E US BUSINESS	$ 160.37	0.0235	14	-	$ 3.77
MC DOMESTIC MERIT III (DB)	$ 135.39	0.0105	3	$ 0.15	$ 1.87
MC DOMESTIC MERIT III	$ 208.34	0.0158	18	$ 0.10	$ 5.09
MC ENHANCED KEY ENTERED	$ 409.35	0.0204	7	$ 0.10	$ 9.05
MC ENHANCEDMERIT III BASE	$ 353.00	0.0173	36	$ 0.10	$ 9.71
MC FOREIGN ELECT PLUS US LOC	$ 25.66	0.0161	2	-	$ 0.41
MC FOREIGN STANDARD PLUS US LOC	$ 4.41	0.0214	1	$ 0.10	$ 0.19
MC KEY ENTERED	$ 25.00	0.0189	1	$ 0.10	$ 0.57
MC KEY ENTERED DEBIT	$ 228.34	0.0164	14	$ 0.16	$ 5.98
MC RESTEURANT DEBIT	$ 683.31	0.0119	34	$ 0.10	$ 11.53
MC SMALL TICKET DEBIT	$1,319.53	0.0155	152	$ 0.04	$ 26.53
MC WORLD RESTEURANT	$ 285.60	0.0173	25	$ 0.10	$ 7.44
MC WRLD ELITE OTHER	$ 47.75	0.0275	2	$ 0.10	$ 1.51
MC WRLD ELITE RESTEURANT	$ 122.12	0.0173	12	$ 0.10	$ 3.31
MC WRLD T&E (DINING TRAVEL AGENT)	$ 42.95	0.023	2	$ 0.10	$ 1.19
VS CPS BUSINESS CARD T&E	$ 212.45	0.024	17	$ 0.10	$ 6.80
VS CPS SMALL TICKET PROGRAM	$ 607.77	0.0165	69	$ 0.04	$ 12.79
VS CPS/RESTEURANT CREDIT	$ 256.67	0.0154	6	$ 0.10	$ 4.55
VS CPS/RESTEURANT DEBIT	$1,037.13	0.0119	51	$ 0.10	$ 17.44
VS CPS/REWARD 2	$ 186.94	0.019	9	$ 0.10	$ 4.45
VS CPS/SMALL TICKET DEBIT	$1,914.01	0.0155	218	$ 0.04	$ 38.39
VS EIRF DEBIT	$ 313.50	0.0175	17	$ 0.20	$ 8.89
VS EIRF NON-CPS-ALL OTHER	$ 73.25	0.023	3	$ 0.10	$ 1.98
VS SIGNATURE CARD ELECTRONIC	$ 109.9	0.023	6	$ 0.10	$ 3.13
VS SIGNATURE STANDARD	$ 17.61	0.027	1	$ 0.10	$ 0.58
VS SIGNATURE PREFERRED-ELECT T&E	$ 16.96	0.023	2	$ 0.10	$ 0.59
MASTERCARD WATS AUTH FEE			329	$ 0.20	$ 65.80
VISA WATS AUTH FEE			404	$ 0.20	$ 80.80
AMEX WATS AUTH FEE			149	$ 0.25	$ 37.25
BATCH SETTLEMENT FEE			31	$ 0.25	$ 7.75
VISA INTL SERVICE FEE			7	$ 0.06	$ 0.44
MASTERCARD ASSESSMENT FEE	$4,085.86	0.00095			$ 3.88
VISA ASSESSMENT FEE	$4,746.26	0.000925			$ 4.39
MMV MONTHLY ACCESS FEE			1	$ 1.95	$ 1.95
MONTHLY STATEMENT FEE			1	$10.00	$ 10.00
US CROSS BORDER FEE			2	$ 0.05	$ 0.09
TOTAL FEES					**$400.93**

Than our rates:

Processor	Volume	Discount Rate	Item Count	Item Rate	Fees
MC COMMERCIAL T&E US CORP	$ 34.74	0.0235	3	-	$ 0.82
MC COMMERCIAL T&E US BUSINESS	$ 160.37	0.0235	14	-	$ 3.77
MC DOMESTIC MERIT III (DB)	$ 135.39	0.0105	3	$0.15	$ 1.87
MC DOMESTIC MERIT III	$ 208.34	0.0158	18	$0.10	$ 5.09
MC ENHANCED KEY ENTERED	$ 409.35	0.0204	7	$0.10	$ 9.05
MC ENHANCEDMERIT III BASE	$ 353.00	0.0173	36	$0.10	$ 9.71
MC FOREIGN ELECT PLUS US LOC	$ 25.66	0.0161	2	-	$ 0.41
MC FOREIGN STANDARD PLUS US LOC	$ 4.41	0.0214	1	$0.10	$ 0.19
MC KEY ENTERED	$ 25.00	0.0189	1	$0.10	$ 0.57
MC KEY ENTERED DEBIT	$ 228.34	0.0164	14	$0.16	$ 5.98
MC RESTEURANT DEBIT	$ 683.31	0.0119	34	$0.10	$ 11.53
MC SMALL TICKET DEBIT	$1,319.53	0.0155	152	$0.04	$ 26.53
MC WORLD RESTEURANT	$ 285.60	0.0173	25	$0.10	$ 7.44
MC WRLD ELITE OTHER	$ 47.75	0.0275	2	$0.10	$ 1.51
MC WRLD ELITE RESTEURANT	$ 122.12	0.0173	12	$0.10	$ 3.31
MC WRLD T&E (DINING TRAVEL AGENT)	$ 42.95	0.023	2	$0.10	$ 1.19
MC DISCOUNT RATE	$4,085.86	0.002			$ 8.17
VS CPS BUSINESS CARD T&E	$ 212.45	0.024	17	$0.10	$ 6.80
VS CPS SMALL TICKET PROGRAM	$ 607.77	0.0165	69	$0.04	$ 12.79
VS CPS/RESTEURANT CREDIT	$ 256.67	0.0154	6	$0.10	$ 4.55
VS CPS/RESTEURANT DEBIT	$1,037.13	0.0119	51	$0.10	$ 17.44
VS CPS/REWARD 2	$ 186.94	0.019	9	$0.10	$ 4.45
VS CPS/SMALL TICKET DEBIT	$1,914.01	0.0155	218	$0.04	$ 38.39
VS EIRF DEBIT	$ 313.50	0.0175	17	$0.20	$ 8.89
VS EIRF NON-CPS-ALL OTHER	$ 73.25	0.023	3	$0.10	$ 1.98
VS SIGNATURE CARD ELECTRONIC	$ 109.97	0.023	6	$0.10	$ 3.13
VS SIGNATURE STANDARD	$ 17.61	0.027	1	$0.10	$ 0.58
VS SIGNATURE PREFERRED-ELECT T&E	$ 16.96	0.023	2	$0.10	$ 0.59
VS DISCOUNT RATE	$4,746.26	0.002			$ 9.49
MASTERCARD WATS AUTH FEE			329	$0.10	$ 32.90
VISA WATS AUTH FEE			404	$0.10	$ 40.40
AMEX WATS AUTH FEE			149	$0.15	$ 22.35
BATCH SETTLEMENT FEE			31	$0.15	$ 4.65
VISA INTL SERVICE FEE			7	$0.06	$ 0.44
MASTERCARD ASSESSMENT FEE	$4,085.86	0.00095			$ 3.88
VISA ASSESSMENT FEE	$4,746.26	0.000925			$ 4.39
MMV MONTHLY ACCESS FEE			1	$1.95	$ 1.95
MONTHLY STATEMENT FEE			1	$8.50	$ 8.50
US CROSS BORDER FEE			2	$0.05	$ 0.09
TOTAL FEES					**$325.79**
MONTHLY SAVINGS					**$ 75.14**
ANNUAL SAVINGS					**$901.63**

We simply left the interchange pass-through plan in place, added our profit of 0.2% on the top of interchange and lowered the authorization fees for Visa and MasterCard from 20 cents to 10 cents per each transaction; AMEX from 25 cents to 15 cents and batch fee also from 25 cents to 15 cents. The statement cost is now $8.50. This way we can save this merchant $75.14 a month and annual savings of $901.63, assuming that monthly volume and transaction count will be close to the one on the statement. This was easy, wasn't it?

When I was doing sales calls, merchants often said that they have a wonderful deal and paid a flat fee of 1.59% or close to it across the board for all the cards, and nobody can beat the price. In many locations this fee was different, and varied between 1% to 1.69%. How do you tell them that the processor can't sell the rates below his cost because he would lose money? When I tried to explain to them that this is not possible, they simply replied that my ISO paid more for interchange and their processor paid less! What arrogance and a lack of knowledge about the industry. But we know that every processor pays the same interchange fees, don't we? There was no way that I could possibly explain to those merchants that they really paid much more for the processing. Even when I showed them the interchange, and the extra hidden fees on their statements, they thought they knew better. They were experts in merchants banking. They surely knew more than me. You will meet those sorts of people, too. When you meet them, do not argue with them. It simply isn't worth of your time. Just leave your information, some literature about the industry so they can learn something and follow up in couple of months. This is another reason why I wanted to publish what I knew, so that merchants can finally get to know the real cost of accepting credit cards in their locations. Remember. The lowest rate does not mean the lowest cost! And you as a merchant want the lowest cost of accepting credit cards not the lowest rate.

If you have some statements at home, you can try to make a comparison based on this formula and see if you can come up with a solution. If you have a problem with the spreadsheet, analyze the above statements and spreadsheets and try to correct mistakes. If it still will not work, ask your ISO or even his competitor to help you make a good accurate rate comparison. Do not forget to get everything in writing before you decide to sign a contract. This way you will be sure that the rates you have are decent.

Now, when you know how to make a true rate comparison and how to read the statements, you can use it on a field visit. If you know how to read the statements, you will be protected from misleading sales reps. Understanding the statements helps you also to understand this business. Step by step, you gain the knowledge necessary to become a successful entrepreneur. If you like sales, you will love merchant banking.

Soon, everything will be electronic. Computers and machines will take over many more aspects of our life as they already have taken. Nowadays, we see more and more electronic payments, check processing and wire transfers. Cash is not used as often as in the past. If you choose to learn this industry, you may become very successful businessman.

It is also crucial for the merchants to understand it. It will help you to deicide where to look for the best processor and how to negotiate the price that you pay for the service. As you all can see, some of the statements and pricing models used by processors are very hard to understand. That is why I recommend you to keep practicing the statements from this chapter until you completely understand them. It will make your work much easier.

Field training

We know the basics, we understand the merchant banking language, we know the pricing plans, how to read the statements and how to calculate the savings. Easy. We have the theoretical knowledge. We are almost there. But there is something that we do not know - specifically how to work in the field and how to close a deal. It is very important to know what you do and what you sell before you go out there to find a potential customer. Some of the merchants will know right away if you know what you are talking about. It is a big plus to know your industry. So now we can concentrate on field training.

Here is where you should start. If you don't have somebody who can drive with you on a field for a week or two, you should take a piece of paper and write down some simple approach that you want to use when doing sales calls. Read it, correct it, memorize it, write down two or more and decide which one sounds better. After that, all you can do is experiment and see which one works. Go out and try some sales calls in your neighborhood. Every time you make a sales call, make a note. Write the owner's name, the next appointment day or when is the best time to come back to talk to the owner. Mark it in your notebook and go over your list at the end of the day. Then, based on the notes plan your next day. After three days of cold calling sit down and analyze your approach one more time. You should know what is working and what is not.

Every sales call is different, every situation is different. You need to be a quick thinker in this business. One time during a sale, the owner of the business told me that I had only one minute to explain my proposal to him. It took me only 50 seconds to say it. I took out the application and closed a deal. It is important to make a good impression. Always. Most sales people fail because they lack field training. They know the business, but they do not know what to say and how to sell. It is the most important aspect of merchant banking - field training.

Here is another suggestion. Talk to your ISO. Ask him to help you with learning the sales skills from one of his best reps. How? Not over the phone of course. Ask your ISO to send his best salesman to drive with you for a week or two. This way you'll learn how to approach the merchant, how to talk and how to close a deal.

The best way to learn is by observation. Being in the situation puts you in different perspective. Makes you think. When you think, you learn. Conference calls might work, but are not as effective. You may benefit from conference calls after you learn how to sell. Otherwise it will be just like listening to a radio show. If you will not make good notes, you will forget about the discussed topic and you will not know how to apply it in the field. I was not able to do any sales calls after my first experiences. Only after I had an opportunity to drive with one of the company representatives I was able to get the encouragement so necessary in the beginning. I also had an opportunity to ask as many questions as possible and practice the sales techniques. Driving with somebody who knows the business is very motivational. It helps you to focus on your work and to master your sales skills.

I think if I had my own ISO, I would drive myself with my reps for couple of days to encourage them or at least call them once a week. But if my sales force would grow to couple of hundred people I would hire a regional manager who would be visiting my reps every month to help them with signing more merchant accounts.

It helps to establish a great relationship with your sales reps - the new ones, and those who have been working for years. It helps them, and it helps you to be more focused. You might even learn from the reps and their techniques. Everybody needs encouragement from time to time. This is a tough industry and if you can't make a sale you can get discouraged very fast. Whatever you do, do with passion and you will succeed.

> *"Logic will take get you from A to B. Imagination will take you everywhere"* – Albert Einstein.

Use your imagination and you will be able to close every deal.

Sales calls

The hardest part for every merchant level salesman is to get the motivation. I have had my ups and downs during my past two years of selling. After visiting around 35 locations a day, setting appointments with the business owners and doing hundreds of presentations sometimes I still could not close a deal. I came home empty-handed late at night with no contracts. I really was getting depressed. But I kept going back to talk to the same merchants - I talked with some of them 20 times. I knew from my past sales experience not to give up. Selling is not easy, especially in merchant banking. You need to perform in order to make a sale. You do not perform, you do not make a sale, no sale, no money. You starve. You starve to make a sale. But it is important to stick with it if you want to succeed. Keep selling. There is always somebody who will buy from you sooner or later. Be patient. It will pay off.

Merchant banking is just a simple mathematics. The more money you process the more money you make. It is the same thing with the number of locations that you visit. The more merchants you visit, the more contracts you sign. To be successful you really need to visit around 30-40 locations a day. It's important to remember to follow up those visits - even if you feel unwelcome. Follow up, even when they say "no". Buy them coffee and donuts. And keep going back to see them. Yes, this way you will make them feel that they owe you at least a good word.

And keep coming back until you get the statement, than sign the account. It is a very hard work. It takes a lot of sacrifice and patience. You might need to swallow your pride from time to time. If you do not like it, go and find another line of work.

Many sales people never go back to the same place twice. Big mistake. Always follow up even if you need to go back to the same location 30 times to see the owner. You say it is too far to drive? Get on the bus. It will save you some driving. First the manager will get to know you, then he will become your friend, then you get to know the staff and then the owner will finally say yes! to your proposal! He'll know that you are a serious businessman.

I visited one location, a lumberyard, about 50 times. Every time I was in the neighborhood, I just walked inside to say hello or to bring coffee for the management. Most of the times I talked to the bookkeeper. I was analyzing her statements, going over the numbers with her, explaining the Interchange Fees and educating her about the industry. I simply shared all my knowledge with her so she could have a better understanding of my proposal. It was a long sale. I felt like I was a tutor and the bookkeeper was a reluctant student. But I was patient and very professional at all times. I always answered all the questions and explained the meaning of it. Persistence pays off. Finally I signed the contract with this lumberyard. I did not take no for an answer and earned myself a trust of the owner and established a good relationship.

Every time a new salesman approached the lumberyard's owners, they simply gave him my cell number so they could talk to me. It was actually very funny. I asked the salesman questions about the interchange, annual fees and termination fees. Just imagine what was going on in my competitor's head when I said that I wanted to pay 2 basis points over interchange with no annual fees, termination fees etc and I wanted everything in writing. The bottom line is that the owner was very loyal to me, because he saw that I strongly believed in my product and I was very dedicated to my work.

The lumberyard remains a good account with monthly processing volume of around $220,000 in Visa and MasterCard transactions alone. The management calls me from time to time asking me just to stop by. Those deals get you back on track and you find your motivation again. When I caught the momentum I could close three deals a day! But those three deals reflected many weeks of work. My ISO asked me how I managed to do three accounts a day! I always told him that hard work pays off.

> *"With a man there is nothing better than that he should eat and indeed drink and cause his soul to see good because of his hard work..."* (Ecclesiastes 2:24)

There is no better training than doing sales calls on your own. I developed my own technique of selling, I started to use a specific approach for most of the merchants and it started to work.

Every night when I came back home, I went over the list of the locations that I visited during the day and the past week and made myself a list of places to visit for the next two or three days. I recommend that you to do that too. This way you will always have a plan for the next couple of days. Remember, that the key to success is to always be prepared. Do your homework. It will make your sales easier. It will make your life easier. I hate to wake up in the morning without any plan for the day. It is the waste of life! Waste of time. So remember-be prepared for the next day.

I was concentrating mostly on the merchants I talked to and who were at least a little interested in my product. I did not waste my time. When I went to visit a merchant who was a little out of the way, I always parked my car for around two hours and made another ten to fifteen sales calls around his location to gain a potential customer. After a while I managed to have seven accounts on just one street. You can't imagine how easy it is to sell the account when you approach a business owner and you say to him that half of his neighbors were processing with me.

Here is one of the approaches that I used:

> Mr. Merchant, I am a local merchant banker, I process credit card transactions. I am different than most of the processors on the market. First of all I do not charge you any termination fees, monthly minimums, monthly service fees and any annual membership fee and you get everything in writing! I simply pass my cost of the transactions directly to you, so you can buy the product straight from Visa and MasterCard and I make only .30 cents on every $100 that I process for you. It means that my company makes $3.00 on every $1000 processed at your store. Here is the Interchange, please take a look at it and visit Visa's and MasterCard's Web sites to compare those rates. If you can show me your statement I can make to the penny comparison and show you how much money I can save you per month. I give you such a great price because I want to keep you as my client forever.

If the merchant said he didn't like changes I always answered that the change is good! Change makes the world goes around! We see changes in our lives all the time.

If this approach still did not work after a second visit, I always added: *If you are really not sure that my deal is so good, let me process for you for a month and then you will deicide for yourself if my rates and service are really better. If you are not happy at the end of the month I will take back my terminal and there will be no termination fee. But if you do deicide to do business with me I will help you to cancel the contract with your past processor.*

I am just giving you an example. You may have a different approach and it might work much better. I am just telling you what has worked for me.

The reason I used the Cost Plus pricing is simple. I was absolutely positively sure, that I would never lose money on the account. I could set the goal of how many accounts I needed to close to make a specific income and made sure to calculate that the ISO paid me what I deserved. And I was always honest. No lies. This is very important.

It worked in most of the places. If it did not work, I kept coming back, because I knew that one day this merchant would give me a chance to take a look at his statement and the rest would be very easy. Persistence one more time.

Never give up. Just keep moving forward. How hard are you willing to work to sign the account? Are you ready to visit the same merchant over and over again to earn his business? Colossians 3:23 says: "Whatever you are doing, put your whole heart into it, as you were doing it for the Lord and not for the men" *(The New English Bible)*. Great advice. There is always something happening with the credit card terminal and if you will keep visiting the same merchant, you will sign a deal. Some of you may not agree, and say that this is a waste of time. Nothing more mistaken! Every time you visit the merchant he gets to know you, remembers you and finally gets to like you. At the end the merchant learns to trust you, and than he signs the contract and in some cases you get a referral. The best time to sign the account is the end of the year - that's when. Most of the credit card companies charge the merchant annual membership fee. This is something that the merchant in most cases is not aware of, and when you point it out to him, you close a deal. Nobody likes to give up the money for free. All you need to do than, is just to look at the bigger picture. Just tell the merchant that by signing the contract with you, he is automatically saving $70 annual fee, then bring down the discount rates and the merchant will have some extra monthly savings.

Of course, the merchant potential savings depend on a monthly volume. The bigger the monthly volume, the bigger the savings. If the merchant has a contract and the termination fee, he will get his money back by saving with you. It makes sense.

A contract for two more years means two more annual fees plus higher service fee. Termination fees are usually around $200-$295, but some companies charge even higher termination fees. Merchants usually get this money back after 6 months and then they have just clear savings! And the comfort of not having any termination fee! This is how you start to build the loyalty of your customer. You do it by having no termination fee. Those of you who think that termination fees can stop the merchant from changing the processor are mistaken. Did it stop those who already left you? It just puts this discomfort on your customer and makes him to find a deal that he can easy get out from if he needs to.

If you want to be successful in any sales, first and foremost you need to know your product. You need to know how to sell your product. You need to know how to describe why your product is better than the competition. *And the most important you need to believe in your product!* If you do not believe in your product and what you sell, you will not believe that it is better, it means that you really do not know your product. You need to think that your product is better even when it is not. The best product cannot be sold without a good salesman. I believed in my product so strongly, that I was willing to give the one month service trial for free. I believed in my product because I had a very strong relationship with the CEO of my company and I knew that he was willing to back me up anytime.

Make sure that you can have this relationship. It helps you to feel important. It builds your confidence. You know that you can count on his help with the big deal. How many of you can call your CEO to get him on the phone with the merchant trying to close a big deal? Probably not too many. Just imagine when you say to the prospect whose monthly processing volume is about one million dollars a month that you are going to put your CEO on the phone in this very moment, so he can get a special deal if he decides to sign the contract now! Priceless. You really deserve to have a relationship like this.

You are the one who works hard every day to close a deal, you are the one who brings the business to the company, you are the one who needs the encouragement from time to time to get back on track.

The merchant who can talk to the CEO of your company would feel very important. He would get a better feeling about you as well. This I call customer satisfaction. Price is not always the most important issue. You need to learn that some of the merchants out there do not care about the price as much. If it is good, they are happy, but you need to know some other things. Service is something that they are looking for and if it comes with a better price they will take it without thinking twice. Some of them simply do not like their current processor or the salesman, but do not have enough time to look for another one.

There is always some opportunity for you out there but you need to go and get it. The key to success is the volume. The more locations you visit the more chances you have to sign a deal. The merchant will not knock on your door to ask if he can sign a deal with you, you need to go out there and spend some time to find those, who are waiting for somebody like you.

You have the power to become your own boss, to set the goal, to execute it and at the end of the month you can sit down and analyze your mistakes and correct them. Always make sure that you correct your mistakes. Master your skills to perfection. It is only up to you how many deals a month you can close. Merchant banking is the only one industry that offers you so much freedom and endless opportunity. It is only up to you what you will do with it.

No matter what happens, do not get lazy. I was working in the rain and snow when one of the merchants sad: *You are working even on Saturdays? In the rain?*

I replied: *I am working, because I am different than all the other guys out there. You can be sure, that even when you would have a problem with your credit card terminal on Sunday, you can call me and I would show up to help you.* And he did.

A merchant called me on Sunday just to check if I pick up my phone. I always pick up my phone. And you should too. This way you will never lose a customer or potential customer. They can call the help desk, but it's not the same. You should talk to them first when they call you and than tell them to call the help desk if you can't help. But don't forget to visit them or to call them the next day to make sure, that the problem is solved. This is simply a good work ethic, and it is hard to find in this business.

Always be honest with your customers. It's the only way you can earn their business. If just everyone would be honest, we would not have so many problems in every aspect of our lives. I know that most of you are struggling to close a deal and your monthly residuals do not look too impressive, but if you can build your clientele based on honesty you will win in a long run. Not only they will never leave you and you will earn a steady income, but they will also give you referrals! You will always be able to use them as one as well. I did. I gave my prospects a couple of phone numbers to my clients, so they could call them and find out about my service. If you are sure that your clients will give you good references do not be afraid to leave their number with your prospect. How many of you can do that without fear? Believe me, if you can use your customers as a reference, it is priceless. It will help you to close many important contracts like for example, a bank.

CHAPTER FOUR

SIGNING UP A BANK

There is nothing better than signing up your local bank as your agent! How many of you have ever thought about that? After my first month in this industry I got an idea to sign up my local bank to process for every one of its customers.

A difficult task? Not really - in fact, it's easy. And it puts you on the map right away! Just imagine that the bank has 100,000 customers. You sign a bank, you might get a chance to process for all of them! The bank sends you a referral and you sign the account. It's that simple. And your portfolio keeps growing fast. If the bank does the processing for some merchants through some other Independent Sales Organization, you will need to visit all of them and ask them to sign a new, better deal with you. Many banks do not have the relationship with any ISO. Good. It will make the bank to sign a deal with you faster. ***The bank needs you!***

Here is what I did. First I went to the local branch of my bank and talked to the branch manager. You can do the same, but you have to work for it. First, be professional at all times. Never wear jeans when you do merchant banking. Be confident. The bank in most cases does not know anything about the processing even if the CEO pretends that he or she knows. You have the upper hand.

You have the knowledge to help the bank bring in more business, and believe me, they value this partnership. I found out much information that I needed from the manager to be able to make an appointment with the decision maker.

Remember - always find out who the decision maker is and talk only to him or her! It is important, it saves you a lot of time. When I knew who I should talk to I visited the main office and made an appointment with the Chief Executive Officer and Chief Lending Officer of that bank.

My appointment was set up one month later so I had plenty of time to prepare my presentation and explain why it was in the banks interest to work with me.

My presentation was simple. It was two pages — one of them illustrated the benefits that bank and its customers would have by processing with me, while on the other page I wrote the businesses from the neighborhood that I already processed for, so the bank could call them and find out about my company, service and the relationship that I already had with my clients.

So you see why every aspect of your business is important. If you have a reputation for providing bad service and a bad price, if you never pick up your phone, you will never get to the top and you will never be able to use your customers as a reference. If even one out of ten customers gives a bad referral, it reduces the chances of getting a bank as a new client. I know. You can never make everybody happy, but you can try.

Here is how it works. Every small bank has a relationship with some Independent Sales Organization. It is not profitable for a small bank to take care of the credit card processing for couple of hundred customers. The yearly fees are high, the bank does not have enough resources, not enough customer service, not enough knowledge to pull it off and it is an extra headache. **That is why the bank needs you!** The bank needs you to be able to offer this extra service to its customers. And there is nothing more important to the bank than being able to offer the local merchant service to its customers. The bank makes only some small percentage from the processing part.

But what really makes the bank to look for a processor in the first place? That's easy to understand. In today's competitive market, with so many banks on every corner, it helps the bank to attract merchants. This way the merchant keeps his money there and the bank makes money on different services. It is a one stop shop for the merchant. Processing helps the bank to gain the extra customers. And here you come to play. If you can sign up a bank as your agent, you get every merchant that is processing with that bank right away as your client. All you need to do is to visit those merchants and let them sign a new contract with you. And that is not all! Every month the bank will continue to send you new referrals with the businesses that need your services. Nice! You don't need to make any sales calls anymore!

Almost every merchant that the bank sends you is a guaranteed deal! And you do not need to necessarily beat the current price. All you need to do is to service those clients. And remember to give them a good service. A happy customer makes the bank happy, and it helps to grow your portfolio and your bank account! If you sign up about 90% of the deals that the bank sends you, you will benefit from this partnership for a very long time. But let's get back to how it is done. You can say good bye to cold calling!

So, you have an appointment and you are prepared for your presentation. Now what? Review your proposal and make sure that you can have your CEO on the phone the day of your appointment in case you need a back up. Why? Because 99,9% of the time it helps to close a deal. I always had my CEO as a back up during the negotiations with the banks or the big merchants. You have to be prepared in case your prospective customer asks questions that you can't answer. What would you do if you didn't have your CEO on call to help you? Rescheduling the appointment would drastically decrease your chances of closing a deal. So make arrangements to let your CEO know about the time of your meeting, so that he or national sales manager can be available if needed on the phone. Can you picture the face of your prospect when you say: *let me call the CEO of my company, so he can help me to answer that question!* Priceless. You've already made your potential client feel very important and you've shown that you mean business. Just simply call the office and ask for help.

What next? Well, later you just need to be patient and follow up with the bank every two weeks. I even attended the bank's banquets. The CEO of the bank certainly noticed - he told me that I was everywhere he went. I wasn't stalking him - honest! I was simply involved in the community and showed my face everywhere when something was happening. But we will talk about the networking in the next chapter. Don't be afraid to put some pressure on the decision makers by reminding them that they are losing many customers by waiting.

Just tell them how many accounts you have signed the past month. It will speed up the process. Don't cite specific numbers when it comes to what percentage the bank will get from the referral. Leave it to the CEO, but always make sure that you will see the contract.

Banks are great for the referrals. Those of you who have signed a bank know that. But remember that you don't work for the bank.

Make it clear from the very beginning. It will make this partnership much easier. Have a meeting with the bank officer and his or her staff every month to improve your cooperation. Keep them updated about all the accounts that you opened for them and those who did not sign a deal. The bank has big expectations. If you don't meet them, it will be a painful partnership - but only from your end. The bank will find another ISO and move forward after some time. So keep the bank happy, so you and the bank will benefit from this partnership for years to come.

After you sign the bank, prepare some referral forms with your fax number on it, so the bank can send every deal directly to you, not to your ISO. Be sure that you are the one who goes out to sign a deal. Merchants will get to know you, the bank will get to know your sales skills and work ethics, and after a couple of months your position with the bank will be very strong and your partnership cemented. And remember. Never get lazy because it's easy, and very possible, to lose everything in a single day. And the crush always comes when you think that you are on the top. Keep up the good work and you will benefit from it for a very long time.

I signed my first bank after 14 months of selling merchant banking. Two months after that, I signed another one! And now I am working on another two. If I could do that, you can do it too. Go ahead and make the arrangements with your local bank. Share with them your knowledge about merchant banking. Teach them this industry! You might have a very good chance of succeeding in starting a new partnership with your bank.

In October 2008 I went to Hawaii. I had a pleasure to meet a successful salesman who worked in the same company. He opened about 300 accounts in six years. But when I told him about the banks that I signed he couldn't believe it. He told me that it was impossible to sign a bank because every bank does its own processing. Bad thinking. Only some of the big banks do that. His thinking is not uncommon - many people simply assume things which aren't true. That is why so many of them fail. They have no faith in success. Believe in your success! And you will succeed. And remember. Banks are easy!

Networking in the community

Networking within your own community is vital for success. Let the people know you. Let them know about what you do. There is nothing better for the merchant than a local service. Join the local business club, attend the community meetings, any meetings, political meetings, charities you name it. You'll meet people who may be potential customers, and, by the way, you'll enrich your life as well.

I joined The Pulaski Day Parade and a local Chopin Choir. I sang every Monday for two hours, started to attend political affairs, Christmas parties and charity organizations. And you know what? People started to know me, started to recognize me, started to be interested in my profession. The more people you know, the more people know you and they know somebody else too. Social networking is critical to your success, and to your growth as a person as well as a salesperson. And this sort of networking is a lot easier than cold calling. There will always be somebody who will be interested in your services, and there will always be somebody who will like you and recommend you. That's free advertisement.

If you like to talk, networking should not be a problem. But there's more to it than simply chatting up somebody. Remember to always stay in touch with your new friends. Visit their business once a while. Send them a holiday card. But don't be too pushy. They know what you do, and soon they will be asking you to look at their statements. The rest will be history. You will earn yourself very loyal customers.

You might wait up to two years to close an account, but when you finally sign them, you will never lose them. And remember to give your prospects a decent deal. Some salespeople won't give a better price once the deal is closed. Sure, you have the account. But for how long? The key to success is to sign the account and to have the negotiation skills to keep it. You can match the current price that the account has, but I prefer always to bring it just slightly down. This way you make a customer happy and you eliminate problems down the road. Let them know how much you make on their account. It will make your customers feel better. For example if you make $45 per month on their account, your customers will recognize a competitor's false claims if he says he can save them $100 per month. Be honest. That is the most important service that you can offer to your clients. Always educate your customers. They will value your relationship. Only the bad and greedy salespeople do not educate merchants, so they can get away with a big profit from just one account.

Greed is the root of all the evil: "For the love of money is a root of all sorts of injurious things, and by reaching out for this love some have been led astray from the faith and stabbed themselves all over with many pains" (1 Timothy 6:10). Isn't it true? Many sales people who overprice an account eventually will lose the customer, wasting all the work that they went into the relationship. I prefer to make less, but have many customers and steady income, than to look for new clients every month due to a lost merchant because the price was too high. Build your portfolio by four to five new clients a month. In three years you might be sitting home and watching your monthly processing volume growing on resource online without doing any sales. If you can get 150 loyal customers in three years, you will earn yourself a steady income for the next five years. Then you can slow down and work less or still work hard and keep bringing more deals. It all depends where you want to be in your life. But if you will deicide to work less, bringing just two accounts a month will be enough to keep growing. And you will have referrals!

The first two years are the most important. That's when you develop your sales skills and your work ethic, which either will bring you success or finish your career before it even begins.

My first year was a success. I was dedicated to my job and to my customers and had built a good clientele. Even after I signed an account and reprogrammed the terminal, I still visited my merchants every month just to say hello. You should do it too. It strengthens your relationship with your customers. This way they are sure, that they are dealing with the right guy. Does your ISO appreciate those extra steps? No. But you need to do it for yourself. This way you can grow your portfolio. Is it a waste of time? I do not think so. I opened 72 accounts, with a monthly processing volume of $1,200,000, and around 25,000 transactions a month, working very hard but only part time. I did visit my merchants every month just to say hello. I was happy. They were even happier. It was just a matter of time to get to 200 clients. I have made many good contacts and had many good prospects for the future. And I had my clients to back me up if I needed them. And I read the Green Sheet constantly, kept studying the industry and trying to always stay updated.

After two more months my ISO decided to sell all of his accounts. I was always loyal, so I had two choices. Sell my portfolio for the multiple that I could not negotiate or to keep my accounts and start to work for a new unknown processor. This is the dilemma that some of you might face somewhere down the road. I made the decision to sell and started fresh. I did not see the contract at all, had no power to negotiate the higher multiple for my portfolio and could not take it elsewhere without having third party selling rights.

I had trust in my ISO and wanted to keep the strong relationship that we had. I got 30 times my monthly income, which was not a bad deal. My ISO sent me a check for it - not a buyer, and there was no copy of the contract. I realized later that selling the portfolio by my ISO was the part of the bigger plan. He wanted to grow bigger.

After I sold my portfolio my ISO announced that he had a great new program that he developed and explained to me shortly how it worked. I was very excited to start using this new selling tool. I got to work once again but for some reason I did not use the new program that my ISO talked about. I hit the streets hard and opened 50 accounts in the next 10 months, signed two banks as my agents and open additional 35 accounts for one of them totaling monthly processing volume of $1.4 mln and more than 30,000 transactions. Again, working just part time.

After just 10 months I got back to the higher monthly processing volume that I had before I sold my portfolio and the higher number of transactions. On the top of that I had two banks working with me! From now on it could be only easier! Banks were generating about 6 leads a month; add the deals that I could sign and you have a formula for a success! I could easily open about 100 accounts a year if I wanted to perform. This industry creates great opportunity and at the same time gives you so much freedom. You as a salesman set your own work hours, you are your own boss, you can implement your own strategy and you have unlimited earning potential if you are a hard worker. This market is for creative individuals. Unbelievable!

> *"Everything that is really great and inspiring is created by the individual who can labor in freedom."*
> – Albert Einstein

Agent-ISO agreement

There are many Independent Sales Organizations out there and every one of them offers a different opportunities. How to find out which processor would be good for you? Who should you sign a contract with? What is better, the upfront bonuses or steady monthly residuals? What should you look for in your contract?

I'll try to answer these questions. Most of the processors out there are relatively fair. But you are looking for the best, for the processor who can meet your needs. The best way to find out is to ask your potential employee to give you the phone numbers of some of his salespeople and customers to find out how they are treated. You'll find out if the checks are coming on time, what the service looks like and many other interesting things. This should help you to make a decision. You need to know, what your future customers can expect from your office in terms of customer service and what your future partner in business stands for.

Here's some good advice: *"He that is walking with wise persons will become wise, but he that is having dealings with the stupid ones will fare badly"* (Proverbs 13:20). It is also good to get to know your ISO to find out what are his moral standards and work ethic.

The next step would be to sign a contract and to choose how you want to be reimbursed for your work. Do you want to build your portfolio and collect 50-65% of the monthly residuals for all the accounts, or you want to get up front bonuses for every open account, and get to keep 20% or 30% of monthly residuals? This is an easy decision, at least for me. I chose residuals but some of you will need to accept bonuses on the beginning. By building your portfolio slowly you might not be able to meet ends for the first year. But if your portfolio really gets big, you will make much more than with the up front bonus plan. You need to determine what will work better for you. That is why it is so crucial to choose your future ISO wisely. If the ISO is willing to help you and treat you like a partner in business not like a leech, you may be able to change your contract from up front bonuses to lifetime residuals after a year or two, when your portfolio gets bigger. Of course you may need to understand that up front bonuses that you got from you ISO in the past years may need to be deducted from your residuals on monthly basis, which makes a lot of sense. Is your current ISO willing to help you, or he is just abusing your contract and does not want you to succeed?

So, you know who you want to work with and how you want to be reimbursed. What should you look for in the contract before you sign it?

This is an important step. If you do not want to hire an attorney to help you, first and foremost you need to make sure that you will collect a lifetime residuals from every account that you open and you need to know what percentage it will be.

I also mentioned earlier about third party selling rights. Those of you who are in this industry for a long time know how important it is to have the right to sell the portfolio to any company who offers the most multiple for it. Here is the example why. If your ISO decides to sell the portfolio you will not get the most for it if you do not have those rights. Why? Your ISO will sell it and determine what price you should get for it. Isn't it better, if you can explore your options and decide for yourself what price you wish to command? You are the one who worked hard to build it up and you should have at least the first refusal rights. If your ISO offers you a price that you are not comfortable with, you should be able to put it for sale yourself, and sell it to the highest bidder. You can also go back to your ISO, to check if he can match the price, or you can simply keep your portfolio and continue to collect lifetime monthly residuals under the new processor. So remember - third party selling rights or first refusal rights should be in your Agent-ISO agreement.

What multiple you can get for your portfolio? Well, it depends on many different factors.

1. How old the portfolio is. If it is relatively young, 6 months to 18 months you will not get a lot for it. It might be around 18 times your monthly profit depending on the market. If it is older, 18 months plus - you might be able to get more, 20-22 times. Potential buyers like to see established, long relationship that you have with your customers. It makes them feel more secure.

2. The second factor would be the average monthly processing volume of your customers. If you have many merchants with similar volume the risk of losing one does not affect your residuals too much. You still collect almost the same income every month. This portfolio will be worth more than the one with a couple of big merchants with a big monthly processing volume. If you lose one of those, your income drops down drastically. Too big risk for potential buyers. If they lose one of the big customers, they lose a big investment. That is why for portfolio like that you get lower multiple.

3. Pricing plans. This is a very important factor. If you do not charge your merchants: monthly minimums, monthly service fees, annual membership fees and give them three tier or cost plus pricing, you can expect a higher multiple for it. But if you charge all of those extra fees, the risk of losing the account is greater and the multiple gets lower.

There are some other things that decide about the price that you can get for your residuals but I mentioned only the most important ones. You can always ask the experts from merchantportfolios.com to help you get a better understanding of those factors. The rest depends on your negotiation skills. Keep practicing them on the field! It is very useful not only in merchant banking but in every aspect of your life.

CHAPTER FIVE

YOU ARE THE BOSS, BECOMING AN ISO

Let me walk you through the process of becoming an Independent Sales Organization. Here is what you need to know before you start.

First you need to register with Visa and MasterCard, which is required to be able to use their logos and resell their products. Then you need to establish a relationship with the acquirer. Usually, the acquirer that you choose helps you to register with credit card companies. The rest depends on your sales skills. Most of the acquirers need to see the volume. They make money on the transaction fees. In your first year most likely you will need to bring anywhere between 3000-6000 transactions a month to your back end office, depending who you choose for your acquirer and what contract you'll sign.

For example: the acquirer wants to make $75,000 on you in the first year, which is the lowest contract that the acquirer may agree to.

Let's analyze what it would mean for you. I estimated that you would need to bring around 20 new merchant accounts per month with monthly processing volume of $10,000, average ticket of $60 and 170 transactions a month. If a merchant has the lower number of transactions per month you would have to open more accounts. If you fail to do that, you pick up the bill for the difference and you will not survive in this competitive industry. Let's say that the acquirer made $50,000 on you in the first year. At the end of the year you simply have to pay the difference between $75,000 and $50,000, which in that case would be $25,000 to your acquirer.

You can get the names of the acquirers from Visa and MasterCard or you can simply visit The Green Sheet's website to get the information.

I am not going to suggest any particular one. It is for you to deicide what program fits your needs the best and for you to determine where your future merchants would get the best help desk service. Choosing an acquirer is one of the most important decisions that you will make. The acquirer that you will choose will be your future partner in business and your Organization will fully depend on the back end office.

Let's find out about the fees that you will need to pay to the acquirer.

Here is the example of most of the fees that you have to pay to the acquirer:

Fees	
Auth	$ 0.0325
Ticket	$ 0.0300
Basis Points	0.01500%
Account on File	$ 8.0000
Charge Backs	$ 12.50
Address Verification	
Voice Auth	
Batch Fee	
Help Desk	

Authorization fee per each transaction cost is $0.0325 cents. Transaction fee cost is $0.03 cents. It makes it 0.06 cents total on the top of Interchange transaction fee. Also you pay BIN sponsorship fees to the acquirer of 0.015%, which is 1.5 basis points - $0.015 cents per every $100 processed.

Every account on file costs you $8.00 or slightly more, which covers your help desk fee and customer service. Easy. When you sell your product, all you need to do is to include all the fees that you pay to the acquirer and Visa and MasterCard, then decide how much you want to make on this account and simply mark it up. There are some other fees that you might need to pay to the acquirer but those fees are charged only per occurrence, such as charge backs, reversals, ACH reject fee and many more. All you need to do is to pass those fees to the merchant and this way when it happens, you do not pick up the bill.

Here is the monthly fee that you pay to the acquirer for servicing all your accounts:

Merchant Core Processing
Outlet on File (per open outlet per month)	$ 8.0000
Statement (per location/outlet, includes postage) - print & mail	$ 0.4200
Statement Recap (per chain recap - includes postage) - print & mail	$ 0.7500
Statement Reprint (per statement - reprint & mail, includes postage)	$ 0.7500
Statement /Recap — e-mail	$ 0.1500
Statement/Recap — via Fax	$ 1.7000

You also pay $500 for client level system access which includes: batch account maintenance, client line reporting, national change of address and a couple other options. As you can see, the acquirer makes it very easy for you. Back end office takes care of the statements, charge backs, help desk, underwriting the account and the coding and many features are already included in price. All you need to do is to concentrate on sales, programming, office management and logistics. Depending on your relationship with the Regional Sales Manager from your local acquirers office, he might send you some agents from time to time that are looking for ISO's from your area. This helps to build your sales force, which is an important key to your success.

The second step would be to create your own name. The name is very important. Through the name you brand your services and you are recognized through it. I suggest for you to come up with something powerful and easy to remember. This name will become your brand.

Later, you need to meet with your Regional Sales Manager from your acquirer's office to discuss the details. You will find out all about your responsibilities and the acquires expectations, the pricing, statements, reporting tools and all the other necessary things that you need to know to start your business going. This is the most important part. You need to fully understand your responsibilities as an ISO. It is a lot of work and that's why many of you out there would rather work for an ISO than become one. It is simple. You need to work! If you don't perform you lose money, you lose your job and you will need to start from zero again. With the tough competition out there, there is no room for mistakes. You can't just deicide to stay home one day because you don't feel well. There are no excuses. It is a hard work but if you will play the cards well, you may fulfill your dreams.

After you meet with your back end office and learn your responsibilities the time will come to get the training that the acquirer will provide for you free of charge. Depending on whom you choose for your partner in business, training might be a little different. Make sure that the person who teaches you how to fill out and submit the applications also shows you how to apply different card categories for different businesses out there.

Again, if you ask the questions even many times and make good notes it will help you to learn much quicker. Learning how to fill out and to submit the applications to your acquirer will be the key component to your business. It will be the most time consuming work associated with merchant banking. You will gain the experience in time. After you learn it, the time will come to hire your office staff unless you already have somebody. Then, you will need to pass all your knowledge to your management. I suggest starting small at the beginning and having just one or two people in the office who can pick up the phones from the customers and communicate with the First Team while you make your first sales calls marking your own brand name. You will quickly learn that it is harder than before. You will need to close at least 15-20 deals a month or more to be able to survive your first 18 months.

The acquirer tries to help you by extending the time for you to bring the first year minimum income from 12 months to 18 months. Make sure that you use this time wisely. Your ISO's survival depends on it. With some luck after you pay your office staff you may break even or maybe make some money. Of course you might price your accounts above average, which is difficult in today's market, but you should have no problem staying in business.

In a meantime you will master the process of submitting the applications to the First Team, you will find out about all the extra steps of processing those applications, you will learn the underwriting process and you will experience your first accounts being refused approval by the First Team. You will explore the merchant banking industry like you have never before. It is a great adventure and if you can manage the speed it will take you for the best ride in your life, the ride to the top.

After two or three months you'll find out that you will need to build up your own sales force. Otherwise you will not be able to keep up with the appetite of the acquirer. You will need to bring a minimum of 20 merchants a month with average monthly processing volume of $10,000, more or less totaling 3400 transactions a month to your acquirer. With some luck, you can close some accounts that will have 3000 transactions in just one location. It all depends on where you concentrate your sales. For example, most of restaurants and diners have anywhere between 500-3000 transactions a month. You may sign four or five of those a month and you do not have to sweat. Gas stations are another business with high transaction volume. It is the same thing with supermarkets.

Your biggest challenge will be to bring this volume to your back end office. Don't skip any doors. Go after every merchant you can sign. The size does not matter. It is all about the business. The pressure keeps growing because there is no more room for mistakes. You need to work. You need to sign more accounts to survive. Your personal life suffers. Your wallet gets thinner. But there is no room for whiners. That is why most ISO's don't make it through the first year. Do you want to be one of them? Get to work. Work harder. Work even on Saturdays and Sundays. Hire somebody. Teach them this business. With today's market and constantly dropping discount rates it is harder than ever to be competitive on the streets. Even with the value added services like gift cards, check processing, software and business cards you might not be able to attract potential customers. What to do? This is the most competitive industry that you have ever worked in.

The constant changes in the electronic payments make it harder to keep up with it. And it is hard to find good qualified people who understand this industry, because most of them would rather stay with their current ISO. You will have no other choice than to start hiring a new people who have never heard about credit card terminals and will not understand the industry's jargon. Training, then, is the key to success. You start again from the scratch. In order to be able to train your new sales team, you will have less time to sell and brand your own name. You will need to invest a lot of time and money to teach and to train your new sales force hoping that it will pay off. I can help!

Here are just the simple numbers. If you hire 10 people, train them, teach them how to fill out the applications and to close a deal, drive with each of them for three full days to share with them your field experience, than you may be able to survive. Just hope that every one of them will be able to close just one account a month, which should be no problem.

They all have families and friends that have businesses and they may get a chance to open their first accounts very fast. You'll get 10 accounts per month from your sales force plus all the accounts that you can sign. It will be still like the climbing up a very steep mountain but it will make it a bit easier for you. Got it yet? It is still not enough. It is up to you which road you want to choose.

One road is easy but it will never take you to the top. If you take the other, you'll have to kick yourself in the ass every day in order to survive. But that's the road which leads to your ultimate destination.

So now you are an ISO. You survived your first two years. What's next? If you are able to survive your first two years it means that you are almost on the top. Now it will be much easier. Your sales force will bring you more deals and you can concentrate on building your office.

Hire more people, take additional training from the First Team and apply a new strategy to bring more accounts to your portfolio. After your first two years your acquirer will demand that you bring at least 10% more income for back end office each year. It means that if the acquirer made $75,000 in the first year, the next year you need to bring him 10% more, which would be $82,500. This should not be a problem. I know ISO's who, after 10 years in this industry bring around 600 new merchant accounts a month! After your first two years you may finally stop selling and concentrate on building your national sales engine! Yes, you need to think big to grow big and then you'll be successful. You learn to think big through your experience in the field.

First you try to sign up small account, any account just to make a buck. The monthly processing volume does not matter. In that way, you'll learn to trust your own sales skills and improve them. Later, you're not afraid to go after the big, fat accounts because you finally have confidence in your own sales skills. You grow. You start to think big. And not only that — you have confidence in your product. It takes time to get there - which is why many salespeople never complete the journey. They quit. They don't have enough patience. They are simply not committed to their work and cannot stand it when somebody tells them no two hundred times a week! You need to learn not to take no for an answer. You also need to learn when to back up and wait for the right moment. Wait for the right moment and then close a deal.

The merchant wants to sign a deal with you - he just doesn't want to do it on the first meeting. You can learn it only on the field. Gold-Medal Olympic athletes keep training every day even when they already are on the top. They know, that there's always somebody who is trying hard and training more. You can only achieve your goals through your own hard and dedicated work.

Even if you fail, there's no reason to give up or worry. Failure can strengthen your character and allow you to become a master of salesmanship. So if you want to get to the top, you will need to get there by yourself. Nobody is going to help you become a better competitor. It makes no sense.

Here's another lesson. Always have something to say. Never lose your influence on the decision-making part. Don't let anybody make the decision for you. Even, or especially when you disagree with everyone else in the office you should make your point and make sure that it was noticed. Only through your own experience you can strengthen your character and achieve your goal. Leave the day-dreams for the others. They are losers. They will never succeed. You will.

And now some numbers

Are you doing well in mathematics? If not, I will try to help you to understand the numbers.

Merchant banking is nothing more than the numbers - from the point of signing the account to the check that comes to you at the end of the month. These are all numbers. When you are signing a deal you need to know the discount rates and calculate the potential savings that the merchant may get by processing with you. Then, you sit down in front of the computer and watch your portfolio growing. It is all about numbers. Monthly volume, number of transactions and finally your profit.

Merchant banking is based on volume. We all know that to make money in any business you need to sell and you need to sell a lot. The more you sell the more money you make. It is a simple formula understood even in 10th century. All of the big companies out there make money on volume.

Walmart, Costco, any auto industry, supermarket and the bank. Even the musicians. You name it.

The power is in volume. The bigger they get and the more they sell, the more money they make.

The service you offer is needed. Every merchant out there needs to accept credit payments to expand his book of business. It increases a merchant's revenue. And you have endless opportunities! Any business on the market is your potential customer; from the government to small deli stores! And almost every American has at least one credit card or two. That's why I want to describe the merchant banking philosophy using just the numbers.

Below is the commission calculator that shows in the first column the number of the accounts that processor has, second column shows average monthly processing volume for each account, third a discount rate which in that case is 30 basis points over interchange 0.3%, and the last column shows the monthly profit that the processor would generate from those accounts.

Below is a model that I used to explain to you how the numbers work.

New Accounts	Monthly Volume	Discount Rate	Monthly Profit
10	$10,000.00	0.003	$ 300.00
50	$10,000.00	0.003	$ 1,500.00
100	$10,000.00	0.003	$ 3,000.00
200	$10,000.00	0.003	$ 6,000.00
500	$10,000.00	0.003	$ 15,000.00
1000	$10,000.00	0.003	$ 30,000.00
2000	$10,000.00	0.003	$ 60,000.00
5000	$10,000.00	0.003	$ 150,000.00
10000	$10,000.00	0.003	$ 300,000.00
20000	$10,000.00	0.003	$ 600,000.00
50000	$10,000.00	0.003	$1,500,000.00

Do you want to make 0.3%? You can bring the numbers up. It is up to you, as I said before, how much you want to make. You can give yourself a raise at any time of the year. Just bring the percentage up and close more accounts and you make more money. Some processors raise the percentage every year to make a bigger profit. That's why you need to have everything in writing. You need to have a contract, which says that the processor will never increase its profit margins for life of the relationship. This I call a good deal. All of my customers got it.

Processors usually wait when Visa or MasterCard raises one or two interchange categories and they use it as an excuse to raise all of them. That's why as I mentioned before, signed a contract, which says that the profit margins of the processor will never increase. This way you can be sure that even when the interchange goes up, your service price will stay the same.

As you can clearly see, the more accounts you have the more money you can make. Do you think that you can't open 5000 accounts? It's easy. With good marketing and a good sales force you can reach that number in about four to five years. After five years in this industry your sales engine might bring you 150 to 300 new merchant accounts a month! There are thousands of businesses out there that are waiting for a better rate or service. You just need to work hard. If you will have a difficulty training your sales force, hire somebody who knows this business and is willing to help you.

Here is another model that shows how the volume works.

1. First column shows number of your sales professionals working for you;
2. Second - the number of the accounts that one of your MLS's opens a month;
3. Third - total number of the accounts opened by your sales team in one month;
4. Average monthly volume of the account;
5. Fifth shows the total monthly volume of those accounts;
6. Sixth column shows the service fee that you charge every account;
7. Total income that those accounts generate on monthly basis;
8. Finally the last column shows your profit assuming that you take 50% of the entire income.

Commission calculator # 1

Sales professionals	Accounts open	Total number of the accounts	Average volume	Total monthly	Service fee	Monthly income	Your income
10	4	40	$10,000.00	$ 400,000.00	0.003	$ 1,200.00	$ 600.00
25	4	100	$10,000.00	$ 1,000,000.00	0.003	$ 3,000.00	$ 1,500.00
50	4	200	$10,000.00	$ 2,000,000.00	0.003	$ 6,000.00	$ 3,000.00
100	4	400	$10,000.00	$ 4,000,000.00	0.003	$12,000.00	$ 6,000.00
150	4	600	$10,000.00	$ 6,000,000.00	0.003	$18,000.00	$ 9,000.00
200	4	800	$10,000.00	$ 8,000,000.00	0.003	$24,000.00	$12,000.00
300	4	1200	$10,000.00	$12,000,000.00	0.003	$36,000.00	$18,000.00
500	4	2000	$10,000.00	$20,000,000.00	0.003	$60,000.00	$30,000.00

This is, how many accounts your team can open in just one month and the income that they generate. Let's try to see how many accounts your sales team can open in one year assuming that one sales professional opens four accounts a month, which should not be a problem and what would be income you could generate from it based on cost Plus Pricing and service fee 0.3% over Interchange not including transaction fees.

Commission calculator # 2

Sales professionals	Accounts open	Accounts open	Average monthly	Total monthly	Service fee	Total monthly	Your monthly
10	4	480	$10,000.00	$ 4,800,000.00	0.003	$ 14,400.00	$ 7,200.00
25	4	1200	$10,000.00	$ 12,000,000.00	0.003	$ 36,000.00	$ 18,000.00
50	4	2400	$10,000.00	$ 24,000,000.00	0.003	$ 72,000.00	$ 36,000.00
100	4	4800	$10,000.00	$ 48,000,000.00	0.003	$144,000.00	$ 72,000.00
150	4	7200	$10,000.00	$ 72,000,000.00	0.003	$216,000.00	$108,000.00
200	4	9600	$10,000.00	$ 96,000,000.00	0.003	$288,000.00	$144,000.00
300	4	14400	$10,000.00	$144,000,000.00	0.003	$432,000.00	$216,000.00
500	4	24000	$10,000.00	$240,000,000.00	0.003	$720,000.00	$360,000.00

The larger the monthly processing volume, the higher the income. In this model I estimated, that the average merchant account would process around $10,000 a month. The account is priced 0.3% above Interchange and brings you the monthly profit of $30. This is just one account. Imagine if you have 3000 accounts! This would mean $30.00 x 3000 = $90,000 in monthly profit. A good salesman can open around 70 accounts a year. You hire ten of those and you have around 700 new accounts a year! Where does it bring you on my table? It shows me that after a year you make around $15,000 a month! Why? You need to pay at least 50% of that income to your sales force. Every MLS takes anywhere between 50%- 70% of that income, which keeps him happy. A happy salesman brings more accounts! More accounts mean more income! If you take care of your people, they take care of business!

In the real world, the numbers work even better. The average merchant out there is processing about 18,000 a month, which would bring your income up about $24 per one account priced 0.3% over Interchange:

Commission calculator # 3

New Accounts	Monthly Volume	Discount Rate	Monthly Profit
10	$18,000.00	0.003	$ 540.00
50	$18,000.00	0.003	$ 2,700.00
100	$18,000.00	0.003	$ 5,400.00
200	$18,000.00	0.003	$ 10,800.00
500	$18,000.00	0.003	$ 27,000.00
1000	$18,000.00	0.003	$ 54,000.00
2000	$18,000.00	0.003	$ 108,000.00
5000	$18,000.00	0.003	$ 270,000.00
10000	$18,000.00	0.003	$ 540,000.00
20000	$18,000.00	0.003	$1,080,000.00
50000	$18,000.00	0.003	$2,700,000.00

Let's calculate the income for 3000 accounts with monthly processing volume of $18,000 priced 0.3% over interchange.

3000 x $18,000 = $162,000

A total monthly income for 3000 accounts goes up to $162,000 and you take a check for $81,000 every month! If this is not enough, you can collect your monthly residuals until the very last account leaves you. Of course residuals would go down every time you lose a customer. Then you do not make a penny. And do not forget that you also make money on the transaction fees. Every transaction priced higher than 16 cents brings you additional income. If you process 100,000 transaction a month priced 20 cents for a transaction, your additional income would be around $4,000. Let's say that you have 3000 merchant accounts with average transaction count of 170 per month. Let's do the math:

3000 x 170 x 4 = 2,040,000 : 100 = $20,400

$20,400 would be an additional income just from the transaction fees!

To open 3000 accounts might take you about three to four years if you have a sales team of 15 people, but if you work by yourself you can bring about 120 accounts a year or more, depending how hard you work. Your income depends on the price that you give to your clients. I am not saying that you need to charge 0.3% over the Interchange on every account that you sign. You might make even more if you are a financial shark and mark up the price a bit higher. I personally like to keep my merchants for a very long time by giving them relatively low price.

We know how long it takes to open a certain number of the merchant accounts. Now I'll tell you how long it takes to lose them - about ten years. It is hard to sign a deal and usually it is even harder to lose the account if you price it and service it well. But let's say that you lose an account. You could throw up your hands and do nothing, or you can go out and sign up a new account. Every merchant out there is your potential customer. And believe me — you have never been in a business like this. Endless opportunity.

Of course you can play with the numbers and price those accounts anyway you want. The only thing that will change at the end will be your profit, but it will always be the profit. You will be the only one person who decides how much you want to make. Isn't it great? You set the rules and you are responsible for the outcome. The market verifies everything. The hardest part of this industry after you learn it is to make a sale. It all comes down to that point. Some salespeople out there are great in selling liquor or other products but when they try to sell in this industry they simply cannot make it. It is crucial to be able to sell your product. You are not selling anything different than your competition so what makes it so difficult? The price is similar. Service is a little better. Why then it is so hard for some of you to sign the contract? I'll tell you why. You're no different from the others - that's why. You need to find a niche and distinguish yourself from other processors or salespeople - do something that will make you stand out from the crowd. It might be your approach, it might be your service, or it might be just your hard work.

If you're not a good salesman you can just simply visit 40-50 locations a day and will always sign at least one account on every hundred locations that you visit. As I said — *volume again*. In time you will learn to sell. Practice makes you the grandmaster.

Let's analyze it one more time. I'll use a different example now. The first column shows the number of the visited locations, the second the number of signed accounts and I'll leave the rest the way it was before — monthly volume and service price.

I estimated that you should be able to sign around two accounts for every 100 locations that you visit and that you visit 50 locations per day. Of course you need to follow up on a sale and visit previous locations to establish a relationship between you and the business owner. You might not close a deal on a first visit. It happens. But always follow up. This way you might be able to sign a contract with that merchant at some point in the future. I signed some accounts two years after my first visit.

Here is the second table of numbers that shows you your potential number of accounts.

Visited Locations	Signed Accounts	Monthly Volume	Discount Rate	Profit
50	2	$10,000.00	0.003	$ 60.00
100	4	$10,000.00	0.003	$ 120.00
200	8	$10,000.00	0.003	$ 240.00
500	15	$10,000.00	0.003	$ 450.00
1000	30	$10,000.00	0.003	$ 900.00
2000	65	$10,000.00	0.003	$ 1,950.00
5000	100	$10,000.00	0.003	$ 3,000.00
10000	250	$10,000.00	0.003	$ 7,500.00
20000	500	$10,000.00	0.003	$15,000.00

This means, that to be able to sign 300 accounts you'll need to sell merchant banking for 600 long days. It is hard to tell how much you would make, because your income depends on a monthly processing volume and the pricing method that you used for every account. Usually, if you have 300 accounts open, the monthly processing volume for those accounts would be around $5,500,000. A portfolio like that would bring a total estimated income of $16,000 a month.

Don't forget that you as an MLS get to keep 50%- 65% of this profit, which would be slightly more than $8,000 a month. The ISO gets the rest. So to get to that point you need only two years of hard work! Can you do that?

This is just an estimate. But you can use this model as your goal in your first two years and see if you can get there. I opened around 150 accounts in two years working just part time! Work full time and you can easily open more than 200 accounts in two years. But these are just the numbers. As I said, even if you master your sales skills and techniques, you still might not be able to get to that point in just 18 months if you want to be an ISO. If you make the sales by yourself and have your own ISO, you will not need to share the income with your reps but you will need to work harder. You will need to submit the applications, service open accounts, hire and manage the office staff. This will take away from your sales time. But if you do have a sales force at least half of the income will go to them. But don't forget that your sales force brings you extra accounts, so you get to that point much faster and the income that you generate on monthly basis looks a lot better.

So if you work just by yourself, in two years of hard work you might be able to survive in this unbelievably competitive market. And, as I indicated earlier, if you want to survive you will need to work by yourself at least for some time. That is why, I recommend that you find a business partner at the beginning. It makes things much easier if you both perform and both bring the accounts. You can even split the responsibilities. One of you might sell, the other one submit the applications and service the accounts. Even later, after your company gets bigger it helps to have somebody who can take some responsibilities and manage the office with you. It is only up to you how big you want to be as an ISO and what business model fits you best.

The only way to succeed in this industry is to attract merchants to your company. This way you do not have to spend as much time selling. And here I need to mention another point. After you sign the deal you will need to reprogram the credit card terminal and this takes time.

You need to go back to the same location and spend at least an hour to reprogram the machine. You will find yourself in many situations that will need good negotiating skills. You'll need to do more than just sell your product. You will need to learn to submit your applications to the acquirer and reprogram the credit card terminals. I learned to reprogram credit card terminals during my first two months in this industry. Practice. You open many accounts, you get to reprogram all kinds of terminals and you learn it. It is not hard, but some people will not get it anyway. I saw many MLS's who would rather make sales, so they sent somebody else to reprogram a terminal. But it is easy if you have a help desk on the phone. That's why the acquirer gets paid so much. The acquirer provides you with the service support. You simply call the help desk and they walk you through the process.

After a couple of times you can do it yourself. I still call the help desk to make sure that the download will go smoothly. That's why it is so important to choose a good partner as a back-end office. The back end office helps you to build the download file, helps you to reprogram the credit card terminals, gives you support in changing POS configuration and helps you to navigate your transaction processing needs.

The worst to reprogram are the point of sale systems connected via telecommunication lines to a central computer in the restaurants. You will find out that you might not be compatible with some of the POS Systems. It might cost extra money to reprogram such a POS. The best way to do it, is to call the local software vendor and pay him for the reprogramming. I also recommend that you find two or three POS vendors in your area and establish with them a business relationship. Why? Here are several reasons:

1. It will cost you less to reprogram POS if you run into their software.
2. They might start to send you some leads if you pay them the percentage of your income from those accounts.
3. You may use their software for some of your new clients that are looking for POS and make an extra buck.
4. They will not cause you any problems if you will need to reprogram their software at any restaurant in the future that is using their product.

I encountered some restaurants with POS and the vendors were not very helpful. Of course! What did I expect? They most likely had an interest in keeping the other processor running the transactions there. I could not reprogram the terminal myself for couple of reasons.

1. First it might not been successful reprogramming and the merchant would lose a lot of business and I would lose the account.
2. Second, it is a bit complicated if you do not have training and do not know the software.
3. Third, if something goes wrong it might take you many hours to change the configuration to a previous one, so the merchant can process the transactions with the past processor until you can get the expert to help you with changing the configuration.

So, what can you do? Here is my advice. Get to know the local software vendors and offer them a percentage share. It is a win-win situation for everybody. You may even get the extra accounts from them.

There's one other thing. You make money on all the accounts as long as they stay with you.

Isn't it great? You can lose one or two accounts per month, but if you have 1,000 of them it doesn't matter! You still collect your monthly residuals from the other accounts. There is something about this industry that can help you to make money quicker. As I mentioned before you can always sell your portfolio and get anywhere from 18 to 35 times your monthly income for it. Yes, you can get one big fat check. If you deicide to cash out, you can do it at any time. The multiple that you could get for your portfolio will depend mostly on the current market situation. There are other aspects that may affect it, like for example the number of big accounts that you have in your portfolio, the age of your portfolio - the older the better. I suggest that you concentrate on the selling part and then deicide what to do when you get there.

Are you ready to take the steering wheel and take your career to the next level? If you are, don't forget about one very important thing. *Even the best product can't be sold without a good salesman!*

My plan to change merchant banking

Here is my pricing plan, which will bring change to electronic payment industry. Why? Simply, because nobody in this industry has ever tried anything like this before. This plan will completely change the way of selling. There will be no more percentages on the top of the interchange that the processor charges now. It will be just a simple service fee that the processor will charge in exchange for the percentage.

The new merchant banking pricing plan is based on capitation price of the merchant service based on the monthly processing volume generated at the merchant location. Currently every merchant is being charged fees as follows:

1. Interchange fees, Visa and MasterCard Assessment Fees - which are collected by or on behalf of Visa and MasterCard or other card companies or issuers
2. Monthly service fees;
3. Statement fees;
4. Processing fees - which usually are 0.2% to 1.00% on the top of interchange fees. These fees represent the ISO's or processor's profit. Interchange fee means the charge levied or collected by or on behalf of a card-issuing bank for the processing of interchange transactions.

This means that every merchant is paying all interchange fees and a percentage on the top of those fees.

And here comes the change:

My new Capitated Pricing Plan will allow the merchants to have a significant savings based on the model presented below:

1. For every merchant with monthly processing volume from $0 - $10,000.00 cost + $10
2. For every merchant with monthly processing volume from $10,000 - $25,000 cost + $15
3. For every merchant with monthly processing volume from $25,000 - $50,000 cost + $25
4. For every merchant with monthly processing volume from $50,000 - $75,000 cost + $30
5. For every merchant with monthly processing volume from $75,000 - $100,000 cost + $35
6. For every merchant with monthly processing volume from $100,000 - 125,000 cost + $40

Monthly Volume	Estimated Current Price	Estimated Cost of Service	Capitation Price
$ 10,000.00	0.003	$ 30.00	$10.00
$ 25,000.00	0.003	$ 75.00	$15.00
$ 50,000.00	0.003	$150.00	$20.00
$ 75,000.00	0.003	$225.00	$25.00
$100,000.00	0.003	$300.00	$30.00
$125,000.00	0.003	$375.00	$40.00

The cost of service would increase $5.00 for every $25,000 higher monthly processing volume below the $100,000 mark and $10 above $100,000 for every $25,000 higher monthly volume.

This way, merchants would not have to pay the percentage for service based on the monthly processing volume. They would simply pay just a service fee based on the volume with no termination fees, monthly minimums and annual membership fees.

Here is an example:

$100,000 monthly processing volume priced 20 basis points over Interchange is equal to 0.002 * 100,000 = $200 service fee.

The capitated plan charges only $40. Every merchant will benefit from capitated price because monthly volume times even the small percentage being added to the interchange will always be higher than the capitated plan.

The idea of capitation the merchant service is to help bring the cost of the processing fees down and to help to grow the businesses without decreasing a customer service. Capitation might be used for every merchant; every business will qualify for it with no exceptions.

That is my plan. Why should it be adopted? It is easy to understand, clearly lays what the merchant pays for the processing his or her transactions to the processor and for the customer service, brings down the cost of the processing especially for the big merchants and it does not require any special sales skills. You go to the merchant and tell him straight that the customer service with the processing will cost him $10, $20 or more depending on what you will agree, eliminating all of those extra percentages that the merchant has to pay now to the processor and simplifying this way the entire system of fees being charged to your customers.

Of course we can't make every processor use the same pricing plan. If we would, we would not have a free market. Free market gives us choice. Choice is our right. God gave us free will, so we can decide what is right for us and what is wrong.

Seize the opportunity

> "Rivalship and emulation render excellency, even in mean professions, an object of ambition, and frequently occasion the very greatest exertions" – Adam Smith The Wealth of Nations, Book V, Chapter I

I hope you're excited by what you've learned, and by the prospect of becoming a success. You found out how to make money quickly and honestly. You have the information you need to change your career, and your lifestyle. Remember, almost everybody can become an ISO. The opportunity is out there. You can become an ISO in every country in the world.

But becoming a successful ISO will required hard work and a mastery of techniques I've outlined. Remember. Hard work pays off. There are also many sales books available on the market to improve your sales skills. But the best way to become grandmaster in sales is only by practice.

No matter what future will bring, there will be always many opportunities in fascinating electronic payment industry. And it is never too late to start exploring it.

Most of the processors out there will not be happy about me detailing merchant banking information to the public. But there will be many merchant level salespeople, who will use this book to improve their sales skills, to find out how to negotiate the contract with their current employer and to learn merchant banking business. And lets not forget about the merchants. They will be more educated about this industry and it will help them to negotiate the price with credit card companies.

And remember, do not let the world to shape you. You must shape the world around you, and you will succeed.

CHAPTER SIX

THE AUSTRALIAN REFORM OF CREDIT CARD PAYMENTS

On November 1, 2003 Australia adopted new lower interchange fees after a long battle between the credit card associations and retailers. Many say, that it was a very controversial regulation. Soon after the regulation took effect merchants saw a decrease in service fees, simply because the acquirers passed along their lower cost of the credit card transactions. But did the merchants pass those savings to the customers? Was there anybody to check on it?

According to the Reserve Bank of Australia, the very bank which was responsible for the interchange fee reform there is no evidence that merchants passed any savings on to their costumers (Robert Stillman, et.al., "Regulatory intervention in the payment card industry by the Reserve Bank of Australia: analysis of the Evidence" (28 April 2008)).

According to the bank the purpose of this reform was to lower the cost of goods and services sold by merchants to the customers. It did not work. The regulation helped merchants, not the consumers. Now, the average transaction in

Australia is almost equal to one percent, which is about 1.2% lower than the transaction that takes place in United States. Customers in Australia, who pay cash, pay less for goods and services because merchants lowered their cost for those who use this type of payment. If you want to pay with the card, you have to pick up the bill for processing.

Merchants in Australia are now allowed to charge the *surcharge fee* for every credit card payment. This way, the fee that the merchant used to pay for service is passed only to people who use debit or credit cards and not to every customer, as in the most cases in the U.S. But is it really like that? The study showed, that only about 2% of retailers decided to surcharge customers who pay with credit cards and the savings were not passed to the consumers. It means, that not only the price did not go down, but on the top of that, merchants who decide to surcharge their customers make much bigger profit. Credit card brands in Australia cannot prohibit merchants from surcharging customers for credit or debit card transactions and the honour-all-cards is not a requirement. This way the merchant can decide if he wants to accept the card or not, or to choose which card he wants to accept, and which one he does not want to accept.

All Visa and MasterCard interchange fees cannot exceed 0.5% of the value of the transaction, which I think creates a very competitive market for ISO's. These rules do not apply in the U.S. All of these reforms have positive and negative effect on the Australian payment industry.

1. Merchants can discriminate one payment method from the other, this way customers who pay cash may benefit from a lower price than those who use plastic
2. Rewards programs become less popular, because the customers picked up a bill instead of merchants
3. The annual fees for the credit cards are increasing on the cardholders side, because the banks are looking to recoup the revenue lost due to interchange cuts
4. Banks are not the only issuers of credit cards on the market, which opened the market to new providers
5. People think twice before they use their cards, because now they have to pay higher percentage to the card issuers and the processing fee, which makes this payment method less popular

The Australian experience shows that regulation in the credit card industry if not carefully balanced and negotiated, may bring a lot of controversy and harm to merchants, banks or processors. We can lower the cost of accepting credit cards, but the reform has to be negotiated between the retailers and the issuing banks. Let the processors who use acquirers networks compete on the free market with pricing plans, value added services and constantly improving customer service. Only this way will we find an agreement.

Of course, it will be very hard to convince banks to give up billions of dollars of profit that they generate from interchange fees, because they use this money to cover most of their operations and pay the bonuses to their CEO's. But do they deserve those bonuses and what for? Needless to say, banks in the U.S. are having huge problems nowadays and if Congress brings the interchange fees down, the scenario for the banks will not be too promising. Bailout money helped the government make a first step to nationalize the financial industry.

The second step towards a total control of the financial industry will be by controlling the interchange fees. Banks are the only members of the associations who dictate those fees now. If the banks will be owned and operated by the government, the government will have the power to set the interchange fees and there will be no more negotiations. We all know, that we can't negotiate the sales tax and the business registration fees, which we pay to the government every year, and they go up systematically. I do not hear any complaints from the retailers about that. Will we be able to negotiate the interchange fees with government? I do not think so.

In one of the e-mails during my study of the Australian payments reform that I received from the Payments News, Scott Loftesness wrote:

"Obviously, given the significant cut in credit card interchange rates in Australia following the RBA"s decision, merchants saved money on card acceptance costs. What's not clear is whether consumers actually benefited in terms of lower prices".

The European Union made a similar reform to Australian. The interchange fees in EU vary between 0.7% to 1.2%, which I think could be acceptable in the U.S. market.

Why does it matter to us?

The future of merchant banking

We know that interchange reform would harm smaller financial institutions like credit unions and community banks. They would simply lose the revenue they generate from interchange. Let's find out what regulations are prepared for the payment industry and what merchants and card issuers have to say about it.

The government has been trying to regulate the credit card processing industry for several years. After two big card companies American Express and Discover filed an antitrust lawsuit against Visa and MasterCard in 1998 and accused those companies of preventing their member banks from issuing AmEx and Discover credit and debit cards, the government stepped into action and took a closer look at the electronic payment industry. This lawsuit raised some serious questions that needed to be addressed. In my opinion Visa and MasterCard is not without a guilt.

> *"To widen the market and to narrow the competition is always the interest of the dealers..."* – Adam Smith

In a 2007 settlement, after the US Supreme Court ruled that Visa and MasterCard had violated antitrust laws, AmEx ultimately received $2.25 billion from Visa and $1.8 billion from MasterCard. Discover also settled the lawsuit and received around $2.75 billion from both credit card companies. Just analyze that.

There is more news. A new piece of legislation,H.R.-5546 better known as the Credit Card Fair Fee Act bill sponsored by Rep. J. Conyers (D - MI) and Rep. C. Cannon (R - UT) passed the House Judiciary Committee on July 16, 2008 by 19 to 16 vote. The bill did not pass both Houses of Congress and was tabled. But it was recently reintroduced with some minor changes under the Obama administration - sponsored by House Judiciary Chairman John Conyers (D-MI) and Representative Bill Shuster (R-PA) - as H.R. 2695. The bill if it passes, will adversely limit consumer options and reduce consumer spending, which is not what we need with our current economy. We need consumer spending and we need to have the credit available to the people. It also might put salespeople out of work, limit competition and technological innovation. This would be a big hit in our already weaken economy and at the banks. Many people might lose jobs. Processors would have to adjust to the new situation and implement new kinds of fees that would heart merchants or they would simply disappear. As a matter of fact Visa and MasterCard introduced new fees this year in addition to all other interchange categories: MC - NABU fee $0.0185 and Visa's Acquirers Processing Fee (APF) which is $0.0195. MasterCard's NABU fee $0.0185 replaced MasterCard Acquirers Access fee which was $0.005. It is over 200% increase in price. Visas Acquirers Processing Fee replaced its previous transaction fee which was $0.005. Do they already prepare for the reform?

What will happen with the banks, which strongly rely on the interchange fees that they collect from the credit card fees?

What's more, there's another bill related to merchant banking- S 3086, which is currently awaiting action in the Senate under new version - the Credit Card

Fair Fee Act S. 1212. The bill would empower the Federal Trade Commission to appoint three judges to help the merchant to negotiate the discount rates with the processors who will bid for the contract. You can find it in the Section 3 of this bill: ACCESS TO COVERED ELECTRONIC PAYMENTS; LIMITED ANTITRUST IMMUNITY FOR THE NEGOTIATION AND DETERMINATION OF FEES AND TERMS; STANDARD FOR ESTABLISHEMENT OF FEES AND TERMS. I want to know how those judges be able to negotiate the price if they don't know the basics about this industry? It looks like the government wants to open another Pandora's Box of regulation.

The general counsel for Visa, Inc. said: "The retail federation wants all of the benefits of the payments system - guaranteed payment, convenience, risk management, reliability, and increased sales volume - but wants to shift their cost of doing business onto the backs of consumers."

In August 2008 the American Housing Rescue and Foreclosure Prevention Act was signed into law. This law will take effect in 2010 and it requires acquirers to report all merchant debit and credit card transactions to Internal Revenue Service. Based on what I've seen, the merchants cannot do it themselves, and the government needs somebody who can report the merchant earnings to IRS in detail, and to do it for free. Isn't it the merchant's responsibility to report his earnings? It will be a big challenge for acquirers to find a way to report all of the debit and credit card transactions for millions of merchants out there. And it will be very expensive and time consuming. Instead of helping the industry, the government builds obstacles.

The electronic payment industry was the healthiest part of the U.S. financial industry. These bills and other regulations, might soon change the business and reshape the world of electronic payments.

Some senators blame the interchange fees for higher grocery and retail prices. They say that because the merchant has to pay this fee, merchent raises the price of goods to recap the service fee that he or she pays to the processor and at the end we - consumers have to pay a higher price for all goods. I do not agree with those assumptions. The contracts that merchants sign with the card associations strictly forbids such a practice. If the merchant increases the price of goods because of the interchange fee or in other words passes those fees to the consumer, is breaking the law. I need to add here that Visa and MasterCard lowered the interchange fees for petroleum transactions, which helped oil companies and service stations.

These bills are suppose to help the consumers, but they do just the opposite. Merchants with those bills as a law will be able to surcharge customers for credit and debit transactions, which will discriminate this payment method. In addition to that savings that merchant will gain will not be passed the to the consumers.

Lobbyists from merchant associations are trying to influence the Senate to intervene and to help them to lower the interchange fees. Interchange is a delicate, balanced and very complex structure. Lets analyze the scenario when the merchant can buy the interchange fees directly from Visa and MasterCard with the lower interchange. Every merchant would pay lower interchange fees and reduce the cost of doing business. Fact. Would merchants pass the savings to the customers by lowering their prices? That's far from certain, based on the Australian reform. Why share the wealth when they get what they want?

What would happen with ISO's? Will they still be processing and servicing the accounts or will the acquirers take over this part of the job? If yes, it would create a new, more competitive market for ISO's who could offer lower prices and concentrate more on servicing the accounts. If not, the only change the merchant would find, would be the customer service. All free technical support might become very expensive. The ISO's and sales people might be out of work or they would have to adjust to new market and change the business model. It would most definitely change the way that the electronic payments industry do business and hurt the merchants and consumers.

The price that a merchant generally pays for the credit card processing is usually about 2.5% of the total daily revenue. By accepting credit card payments the revenue of every merchant increases on average 35%. Do the math.

> *"In a capitalist society, all human relationships are voluntary. Men are free to cooperate or not, to deal with one another or not, as their own individual judgements, convictions and interests dictate."* – Ayn Rand, "Capitalism, The Unknown Ideal"

And this is exactly what is happening between merchants and processors. It is voluntary relationship which benefits both parties.

Here's my suggestion to the government. Stay away from the payment industry, which is creating so much wealth for everybody: consumers, merchants and financial institutions. But if you need to regulate it, here is what I believe should be done:

Lets start with having the same interchange categories and prices for all the businesses.

Than, lets lower the interchange fees: all of the debit cards to 0.7%; credit cards to 1.0%, rewards cards to 1.2%; all commercial and business cards to 1.65%; and all the other interchange categories to anywhere between 1.1% to 1.5%. This way, the most expensive interchange fee would cost around 1.65%. It would be more than 1% lower than merchants pay now. The difference would be significant, it would create a huge negotiation margins and open a bigger competition between the ISO's. The idea behind regulating interchange fees in the U.S. is to bring down the cost of goods and services provided by merchants just like the Australian Reform was suppose to do. Lets learn from it.

So if Congress wants to regulate interchange fees, they will need to implement new laws forcing merchants to pass the savings that they get from this regulation to their customers. Only then might it work. If the regulation would only regulate the interchange fees without forcing merchants to pass those savings to consumers, we might see much less spending in our already weakened economy.

Regulation also should include the cap for excessive termination fees, which merchants have to pay for early contract termination. This fee should not be greater than $50 just like in Arkansas. In June 2007 lawmakers in Arkansas implemented a new law, which caps early termination fees assessed on merchants to $50 or one month's minimum charge. Why not do the same nationwide? This way merchant would take his business anywhere he wants after even a month if he wasn't happy with the deal that he currently has.

All the nonbank processing companies would have no choice other than to lower the processing costs to be more competitive and to concentrate on establishing better relationship with merchants, by implementing good work ethics and servicing the accounts. This might be the best solution when it comes to regulation of the interchange fees.

This bill with its current version is unacceptable. It is simply price fixing and entirely controlled by the government. I've read through the bills and I agree. If they will become law, the free market of merchant banking will be destroyed. It will become a political economy where all decisions regarding price and service will become the matter of the state. Congress should help to find a solution and should help in negotiations to find common ground between merchants and card issuers, which would benefit the entire market. The electronic payments industry brings so much innovation and benefits to our economy, and I think everybody should be aware of that. I repeat - hurting the electronic payments might hurt everybody else in the end.

With the current bank situation and the government seemingly ready to nationalize the banks, the interchange fees regulation might not be necessary. If the government took control of the banks, it would also have an influence on the interchange fees. And then there will be no more room for the negotiations. I've never seen government lowering any cost of doing business when government has a profit in it. In the past couple of years we have more and more government intervention in every aspect of our economy and in our lives. I wouldn't be surprised if this would happen.

Currently, President Barack Obama signed into law a Credit Card Consumer Bill of Rights – H.R. 627 which is supposed to defend consumers from the excessive rates that they pay to credit card companies. This bill may cause that the lenders will start charging cardholders the annual fees. It will also freeze the credit and cause that the consumers will spend less money on credit cards which will lead to decrease in merchants sales volume. Less profit for merchants, less goods and services for people, less profit for the banks and financial institutions and less taxes for the government. Simple calculation. The more profit everybody makes the more taxes can government collect from the businesses and the nation prospers– in other words this might stop the wealth creation.

Let's analyze the arguments

I'm going to share with you some comments from both sides of the aisle, so you can decide who has better arguments. In my opinion, interchange should be regulated, but only interchange, without mandating what can or can't do the processor or the acquirer. The free market would adjust to new price situation and everybody would benefit from it.

Here is what a Letter from the Electronic Payment Coalition who represents card associations to Congress says about the bill:

> "...Even a cursory read of the bill reveals that this is nothing short of price controls. The bill refers to determining and/or establishing rates and terms 13 times; a full 35 pages of the 45 page bill is dedicated to describing the price control scheme and the price-setting panel..."

Not a surprise.

> ..."We recognize that large retailers and successful small enterprises look for every opportunity to reduce their costs of doing business, but as the Australia example illustrates, asking the government to do it for you is bad public policy that will harm consumers"...

Trish Wexler, a spokeswomen for the coalition said: "We believe that going to Congress and asking for consumers and for the financial institutions to pay is the wrong way".

Very true.

Here is American Bankers Association's comment on that issue:

> "When merchants choose to accept payment cards, they pay a penny or two on each dollar for the ability to accept electronic payments. Retailers, while fully aware of the benefits these services provide, now do not want to pay for it. Rather, they want Congress to intervene to lower a cost of doing business."

A penny or two on every dollar? That is it? As I said before, the key is the volume.

> "Merchants are trying to position this as a consumer issue. But it is the cost of doing business for them. Every cost of business is probably reflected in prices," Sharon Gamsin, a MasterCard spokeswomen.

Gamsin also said, that credit cards allow people to spend more money than cash, which also benefits merchants.

Interesting point.

And some more facts:

> American consumers have many choices when it comes to acceptance of credit and debit cards. There are more than 14,000 U.S. card issuers. There is no one single institution that controls electronic payment marketplace.

Fact.

Josh Floum general counsel from Visa, Inc. said:

> "H.R. 5546 remains an anti-consumer bill that would mandate unnecessary regulatory intervention into a fiercely competitive industry that is benefiting consumers, merchants, and financial institutions."

Yes, the electronic payments industry is the back bone of our economy and everybody benefits from it.

Lets listen to what merchants have to say about it.

Stuart Zlotnikoff, Senior Vice President of National Grocers Association writes in his letter to Congress:

> "Today, there is another kind of "common tyranny" confronting all merchants across the nation: the excessive, growing, and out of control

interchange fees which merchants must pay to the card companies. According to a survey of a cross-section of N.G.A. member retailers, grocers must now pay 4% to 8% of their store sales of card acceptance. Given the historically thin margins for the grocery industry, this is nothing short of a crisis!"...He also states that more than 50 percent of their purchases are made with credit and debit cards.

No credit cards, 50% less sales... 4-8 percent for card acceptance? Time to change the processor.

Here is what chairman of Merchant Payment Coalition - Mallory Duncan says about the subject:

> "This market is broken. It needs transparency and genuine competition. Currently, the only semblance of competition is the battle between Visa and MasterCard to get more banks to issue their cards. And how do they do that? By promising the banks they'll extract more interchange from consumers than the other guy. This is the only market I know of where the parties compete to raise prices rather than to lower them."

Good point, but not necessarily true.

Unfair credit card fees website (www.unfaircreditcardfees.com), which strongly supports the bill and stands behind the merchants says:

> "Visa and MasterCard charge Americans among the highest credit card interchange fees in the world - averaging close to 2 percent for credit and signature debit transactions, compared with only 0.7 percent in the United Kingdom and 0.50 percent in Australia...

That is the fact. But lets not forget about the Australian experience...This is U.S., everything is more expensive here.

One of the business owners said:

> "Retailers are beholden to credit card companies. We've moved so far to an e-commerce model that if I don't accept credit cards, I am out of business".

And that concludes all above. No electronic payments, no consumer spending, no sales and no business. Everything soon will be electronic

AFTER WORD

I am going to leave you here dear reader, and allow you time to digest your thoughts. I hope, that you have learned and understood the complex world of electronic payments and that you will appreciate the hardworking sales people who visit your door every day servicing your merchant account. I hope that you have learned to appreciate the importance of a mutual working relationship that you need to have with your processor for years to come. After becoming acquainted with the rest of this book, I hope that your business continues to grow with every transaction processed.

For those, who will try to become an ISO, I wish you luck and success. It will be a great adventure and a lot of hard work. With millions of merchants out there, there will always be room for great entrepreneurs like yourselves. Good luck and do not forget to study the interchange and use the Bible or your faith as your moral compass. This will definitely help you to succeed.

Here's what is my moral compass:

> "As regards anything besides these, my son, take a warning: To the making of many books there is no end, and much devotion [to them] is wearisome to the flesh. The conclusion of the matter, everything having been heard, is: Fear the [true] God and keep his commandments. For this is the whole [obligation] of man. For the [true] God himself will bring every sort of work into the judgment in relation to every hidden thing, as to whether it is good or bad" (Ecclesiastes 12:12-14).

Mariusz Kapturski

NOTES & REFERENCES

GLOBAL CHALLENGES
1. Ghulam Umar - United Nations Fundation - www.unwire.org Letter to the UN General Assembly

MERCHANT BANKING AS A PART OF THE FREE MARKET
1. The free market - Free encyclopedia
2. Milton Friedman - www.brainyquote.com

BRIEF OVERVIEW
1. Bible - 2 Timothy 3: 16,17
2. Bible - 2 Timothy 3: 1-5

UNDERSTANDING THE INTERCHANGE AND MORE
1. Bible - Proverbs 14: 15

HOW THE TRANSACTION IS AUTHORIZED
1. Authorization - www.creditcards.com/glossary/term-authorization.php

PRICING PLANS
1. Discount rate, transaction fee, batch, settlement- Chase Paymentech Strategic Partner Program

READING THE STATEMENTS
1. Bible - Ecclesiastes 7: 12

FIELD TRAINING
1. Albert Einstein quote - www.goodreads.com

SALES CALLS
1. Bible - Ecclesiastes 2: 24
2. The New English Bible - Colossians 3: 23

NETWORKING IN THE COMMUNITY
1. Bible - 1 Timothy 6: 10

AGENT-ISO AGREEMENT
1. Bible - Proverbs 13: 20

THE AUSTRALIAN REFORM OF CREDIT CARD PAYMENTS
1. Robert Stillman - "Regulatory intervention in the payment card industry by the Reserve Bank of Australia: analysis of Evidence" (28 April, 2008)
2. Gary Jones Senior Information Officer - Information Department Reserve Bank of Australia 65 Martin Place, Sydney NSW 2000 - http://www.rba.gov.au/PaymentsSystem/Reforms/RevCardPaySys/index.html.

THE FUTURE OF MERCHANT BANKING
1. Credit Card Fair Fee Act H.R. 5546 -
   http://govtrack.us/congress/bill.xpd?bill=h110-5546
   http://opencongress.org/bill/110-h5546/show
   http://www.greensheet.com/gs_online.php?story_id=923
   The Green Sheet 2.0 September 08, 2008 Issue 08:09:01

2. Credit Card Fair Fee Act 2009 H.R. 2695
   http://www.govtrack.us/congress/bill.xpd?bill=111-2695
   http://judiciary.house.gov/news/090604.html
   http://www.washingtonwatch.com/bills/show/111_HR_2695.html

3. S 3086 -
   http://www.opencongress.org/bill/110-s3086/show
   http://www.statesurge.com/bills/353500-s3086-federal
   http://www.naconline.com/NAC/GOVERNMENT/CREDITCARDFEES/Pages/CreditCardFees.aspx

4. NABU Fee - MasterCard Network Access and Brand Usage fee which replaced MasterCard Acquirer Access fee;
   http://transfs.com/blog/2009/04/07/network-access-and-brand-usage-fee-nabu/

5. Acquirers Processing Fee - Visa transaction fee
   http://transfs.com/blog/2009/04/07/visa-acquirer-processing-fee/

6. Credit Card Fair Fee Act S 1212 -
   http://www.govtrack.us/congress/bill.xpd?bill=s111-1212
   http://www.govtrack.us/congress/record.xpd?id=111-s20090609-57&bill=s111-1212

7. American Housing Rescue and Foreclosure Prevention Act H.R. 3221
   http://thomas.loc.gov/cgi-bin/query/z?c110:H.R.3221:
   http://www.electran.org/content/view/398/39/ - this site contains the part of the legislation which says about merchant card information reporting.

8. Credit Cardholders Bill of Rights 2009 H.R. 627
   http://www.govtrack.us/congress/bill.xpd?bill=h111-627

9. Ayn Rand - "Capitalism, The Unknown Ideal"

AFTER WORD
1. Bible - Ecclesiastes 12: 12